SMITHSONIAN

Did You Know?

Space

SMITHSONIAN INSTITUTION

Established in 1846, the Smithsonian Institution—the world's largest museum and research complex—includes 19 museums and galleries and the National Zoological Park. The total number of artifacts, works of art, and specimens in the Smithsonian's collection is estimated at 155.5 million, the bulk of which is contained in the National Museum of Natural History, which holds more than 126 million specimens and objects. The Smithsonian is a renowned research center, dedicated to public education, national service, and scholarship in the arts, sciences, and history.

SMITHSONIAN

Did You Know?

Space

Sarah Cruddas

Author Sarah Cruddas

Smithsonian National Air and Space Museum
Education Specialist Ann Caspari
Education Specialist Rebecca Ljungren

DK LONDON
Editor Katy Lennon
Designer Lucy Sims
US Senior editor Shannon Beatty
US Editor Jenny Siklos
Additional editing Alex Cox, Jolyon Goddard, Marie Greenwood
Additional design Hoa Luc, Emma Hobson, Ann Cannings
Managing editors Laura Gilbert, Jonathan Melmoth
Managing art editor Diane Peyton Jones
Preproduction producer Nadine King, Abi Maxwell
Producer Niamh Tierney, Barbara Ossowska
Jacket editor Francesca Young
Jacket designer Amy Keast
Creative directors Martin Wilson, Helen Senior
Publishing directors Sophie Mitchell, Sarah Larter

DK DELHI
Project editor Ishani Nandi
Art editors Nehal Verma, Kartik Gera
Managing editor Alka Thakur Hazarika
Managing art editor Romi Chakraborty
DTP designers Neeraj Bhatia, Vijay Kandwal
CTS manager Balwant Singh
Production manager Pankaj Sharma
Picture researcher Nishwan Rasool
Jacket design assistant Dheeraj Arora

This American Edition, 2021
First American Edition, 2017
Published in the United States by DK Publishing
1450 Broadway, Suite 801, New York, NY 10018

Copyright © 2017, 2020 Dorling Kindersley Limited
DK, a Division of Penguin Random House LLC
19 20 21 22 23 10 9 8 7 6 5 4 3 2 1
001–322922–July/2021

All rights reserved.
Without limiting the rights under the copyright reserved above, no part of this publication may be reproduced, stored in or introduced into a retrieval system, or transmitted, in any form, or by any means (electronic, mechanical, photocopying, recording, or otherwise), without the prior written permission of the copyright owner.
Published in Great Britain by Dorling Kindersley Limited.

A catalog record for this book is available
from the Library of Congress.
ISBN 978-0-7440-3415-8

DK books are available at special discounts when purchased in bulk for sales promotions, premiums, fund-raising, or educational use. For details, contact: DK Publishing Special Markets, 1450 Broadway, 8th Floor, New York, NY 10018 SpecialSales@dk.com

Printed and bound in China

For the curious
www.dk.com

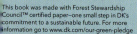

This book was made with Forest Stewardship Council™ certified paper—one small step in DK's commitment to a sustainable future. For more information go to www.dk.com/our-green-pledge

Contents

The universe

8–9	What is space?
10–11	Where does space begin?
12–13	Where did the universe come from?
14–15	How big is the universe?
16–17	How cold is it in space?
18–19	What is an orbit?
20–21	Can you scream in space?

The solar system

24–25	What is the solar system?
26–27	What are planets made of?
28–29	Why is there life on Earth?
30–31	Why is Jupiter striped?
32–33	Is there life on Mars?
34–35	What are Saturn's rings made of?
36–37	Is Pluto a planet?
38–39	How hot is the Sun?
40–41	Why does the Moon change its shape?
42–43	Can it be dark in the daytime?
44–45	Do other planets have moons?
46–47	What would happen if a meteor hit the Earth?
48–49	What is a shooting star?
50–51	Why do comets have tails?
52–53	What is the asteroid belt?
54–55	Can you see the Earth from other planets?
56–57	What are auroras?
58–59	Could you live on Venus?

Deep space

62–63	How many stars are there in the universe?
64–65	Where do stars come from?
66–67	Are all stars the same?
68–69	What is a light-year?
70–71	What is a black hole?
72–73	What happens when stars die?
74–75	What shape is the Milky Way?
76–77	Why do stars twinkle?
78–79	Are there any planets outside our solar system?
80–81	What shines the brightest in the universe?

Space exploration

84–85	How do we look into space?
86–87	Who were the first space explorers?
88–89	Have animals been to space?
90–91	What was the Space Race?
92–93	How many people have been to the Moon?
94–95	How are rockets launched?
96–97	How long does it take to get to the Moon?
98–99	How do astronauts train for space?
100–101	Why do astronauts need space suits?
102–103	What was the Space Shuttle?
104–105	How do astronauts return to Earth?
106–107	Where do astronauts live in space?
108–109	Why do astronauts float in space?
110–111	What do astronauts eat in space?
112–113	What is mission control?
114–115	What happens when things go wrong in space?
116–117	Have we been to Mars?
118–119	Why do we put satellites in space?
120–121	How far have we traveled in space?
122–123	What is space junk?
124–125	Is there anyone else out there?
126–127	What is space mining?
128–129	Can you go on vacation to space?
130–131	Will we go back to the Moon?

132–133	Answers
134–137	Quiz your friends!
138–139	Glossary
140–143	Index
144	Acknowledgments

Discover when I became the first person to go to space on page 86.

Find out why I was sent to space on page 88.

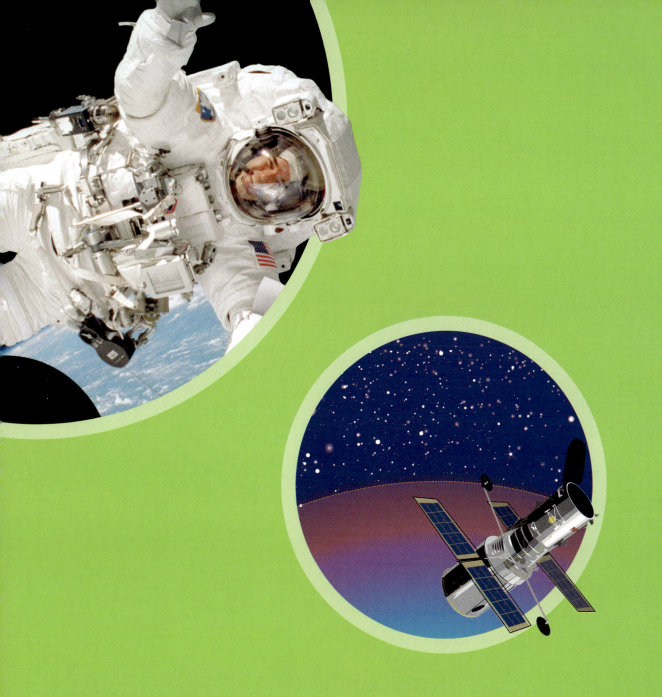

The universe

The universe is everything that we know and observe—from stars and galaxies to all the living things on Earth. We are in the universe right now!

What is space?

On cloudless nights when you look up at the dark sky, you can see space. It stretches much farther than the eye can see and contains the Moon, the Sun, all the planets, as well as the Earth, and the stars. Space also contains many things that we haven't yet discovered.

How do we explore space?

Telescopes
Telescopes help us see far into space. They show us images of stars and galaxies too distant to travel to.

Robots
Robots can visit places in space that humans cannot yet reach. They help us understand these places.

People in space
People have been traveling into space since 1961. During their trips, they carry out experiments.

Since prehistoric times, people have used the positions of the stars to help them navigate.

Giant star cluster
This giant cluster of about 3,000 stars looks like a firework display. The cluster is called Westerlund 2 and is located in the Milky Way galaxy.

Baby stars
Many newly formed baby stars live in this area. It is called a "stellar nursery."

? Quick quiz

1. What is a "stellar nursery?"

2. How long have people been going into space?

3. Is the Earth in space?

See pages 132–133 for the answers

THE UNIVERSE

❓ Quick quiz

1. At what altitude (height) does space begin?
   a) 62 miles (100 km)
   b) 310 miles (500 km)
   c) 373 miles (600 km)

2. What is the second main layer of the Earth's atmosphere called?
   a) Troposphere
   b) Thermosphere
   c) Stratosphere

See pages 132–133 for the answers

First human in space
205 miles (330 km)

Hubble Space Telescope
330–360 miles
(530–580 km)

International Space Station
205–270 miles
(330–435 km)

Exosphere
The exosphere is the top part of the Earth's atmosphere. As you go up, the exosphere gradually becomes the airless environment of space.

Thermosphere
The temperature in this layer of the atmosphere can get very high. However, if you were to travel up there, you wouldn't feel hot because the air is really thin and the heat could not transfer to your body.

Mesosphere

This is the highest layer of the atmosphere in which the gases, such as oxygen and nitrogen, are still mixed up. The word "meso" means middle.

**Aurora Borealis
56–93 miles
(90–150 km)**

**Meteor showers
50–75 miles
(80–120 km)**

Stratosphere

This is the second main layer of the atmosphere and is home to the ozone layer. The ozone layer protects us from the Sun's rays, which can be dangerous.

Karman Line 62 miles (100 km)

Highest skydive 25 miles (40 km)

Airplane height 7 miles (11 km)

Earth

Troposphere

This is the lowest layer of the Earth's atmosphere. It begins where we live, at the Earth's surface, and is where all our weather takes place.

Where does space begin?

It is often said that space begins at the Kármán Line—62 miles (100 km) above the Earth. This is the height you need to reach to become an astronaut. Humans can't survive in space, but are protected by layers of gas that surround the Earth. These layers are called the atmosphere.

What is it like for astronauts in space?

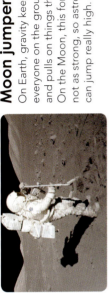

Moon jumper
On Earth, gravity keeps everyone on the ground, and pulls on things that fall. On the Moon, this force is not as strong, so astronauts can jump really high.

Floating around
Astronauts can float and even do somersaults in the International Space Station because there is so little gravity. This condition is called microgravity.

Where did the universe come from?

Scientists think that everything that exists all began to form around 13.8 billion years ago, during an event called the big bang. This started the creation of the universe and everything in it, including us!

Particles form
During the next stage of the universe's creation, tiny particles called protons and neutrons began to form. These make up the center of atoms, which are the building blocks of everything.

Big bang
The theory is that the universe began with an explosion known as the big bang.

Universe grows
After the big bang, the universe grew really quickly and it was really hot!

Matter formed
Within the first second after the big bang, the universe started to cool down and matter began to form. Matter is the stuff that everything is made of.

How do we know how old the universe is?

Universe math
Scientists are able to figure out and guess the age of the universe by studying how fast it is expanding today. They can also look at the oldest objects in space, which helps them to find out how things were made and when.

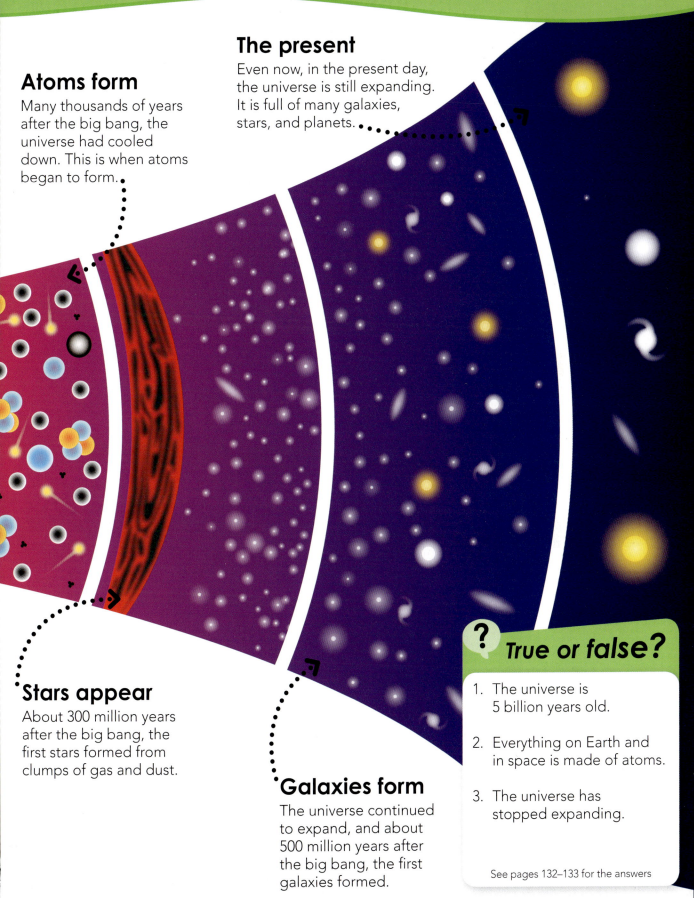

Atoms form
Many thousands of years after the big bang, the universe had cooled down. This is when atoms began to form.

The present
Even now, in the present day, the universe is still expanding. It is full of many galaxies, stars, and planets.

Stars appear
About 300 million years after the big bang, the first stars formed from clumps of gas and dust.

Galaxies form
The universe continued to expand, and about 500 million years after the big bang, the first galaxies formed.

True or false?

1. The universe is 5 billion years old.

2. Everything on Earth and in space is made of atoms.

3. The universe has stopped expanding.

See pages 132–133 for the answers

How big is the universe?

The universe is really, really, really big! It is so huge that it is difficult to imagine the size of it. Our Sun, which is the biggest object in our solar system, is like a speck of dust when compared with the vastness of the universe.

As far as we know, the universe does not have an edge.

The Milky Way
One of the galaxies in our universe is the Milky Way galaxy. There are billions of stars in the Milky Way, most of which have planets that orbit around them.

The universe
Our galaxy is just one of billions of galaxies in the ever-expanding universe. This image shows just a small part of our universe, filled with galaxies.

How big is...?

The Moon
The Moon is our closest neighbor. It might look big in the sky, but it is much smaller than the Earth. It is about a quarter of the Earth's size.

The Sun
The Sun is the biggest object in our solar system. It is so huge that more than one million Earths could fit inside it.

Earth
To us, the Earth seems huge. More than seven billion people live here! However, compared to the biggest planet in our solar system, Jupiter, the Earth is actually very small.

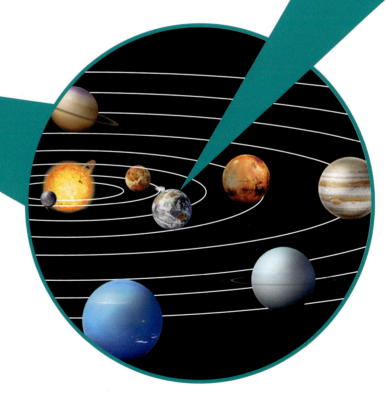

Our solar system
Our solar system is in the Milky Way galaxy. It is so large that if you were to travel to Mars and look into space, Earth would appear like a small star in the sky.

? Quick quiz

1. What is the name of the galaxy that the Earth is in?

2. Roughly, how many Earths can fit inside the Sun?

3. What is Earth's closest neighbor in space?

See pages 132–133 for the answers

16 THE UNIVERSE

Do other planets have summers and winters?

Uranus
Uranus has four seasons that last around 21 years each. The planet spins on a very tilted axis. This means that during summers and winters, the summer side of Uranus is in daylight for 21 years and the winter side is in darkness for 21 years too.

How cold is it in space?

In the huge areas between the stars and galaxies, space can get very, very cold. In these regions, the temperature can drop as low as -454°F (-270°C). However, the objects in space, such as stars and planets, can be lots of different temperatures.

The Sun
This is the hottest object in the solar system. The surface temperature of the Sun is around 11,000°F (6,000°C). Too hot to ever visit!

Supernova
When a huge star explodes, it can become a supernova and temperatures can reach up to 99,000,000°F (55,000,000°C).

Venus
The hottest planet in the solar system, Venus has a thick atmosphere that helps the surface reach temperatures as high as 880°F (470°C).

Earth
The average temperature on the Earth is around 59°F (15°C). However, this can change depending on the seasons and the location on Earth.

Boomerang Nebula
Thousands of light-years away from the Earth, the Boomerang Nebula is the coldest known object in the universe. Inside this gas cloud, temperatures can be as low as -458°F (-272°C).

The Moon
The Moon is a world of extreme temperatures. In the sunlight, it can be as hot as 253°F (123°C). The coldest parts can reach -387°F (-233°C).

Neptune
Temperatures on Neptune average about -353°F (-214°C). Its largest moon, Triton, is even colder, with temperatures dropping to -391°F (-235°C)!

? Quick quiz
1. Which is colder—Neptune or its moon, Triton?
2. What is the coldest known object in the universe?

See pages 132–133 for the answers

THE UNIVERSE

What is an orbit?

An orbit is a path that one object in space takes around another. In the solar system, the Earth and all the other planets orbit around the sun. Also, many planets, including the Earth, have moons that orbit around them.

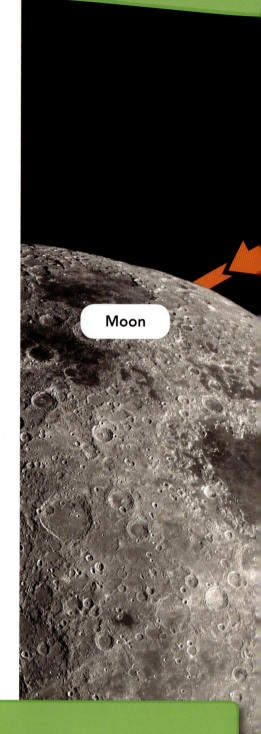

Moon

What keeps the Moon in orbit?

The Moon stays in orbit around the Earth because of the force of gravity. The Earth's gravity pulls the moon toward the Earth, stopping it from escaping into space. Without gravity, the universe would not exist—it is the force that made pieces of rock, dust, and ice clump together to form planets, moons, and stars. It also keeps all the planets in orbit around the sun.

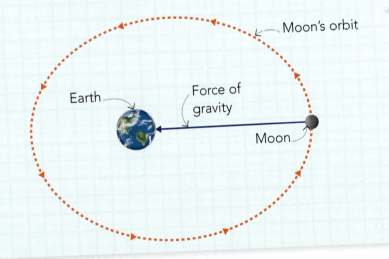

What else orbits the Earth?

Satellites
Lots of human-made satellites orbit around the Earth. This includes the International Space Station where astronauts live and work.

Eye in space
The Hubble Space Telescope orbits around the Earth. It can look far into space and takes amazing pictures of distant stars and galaxies.

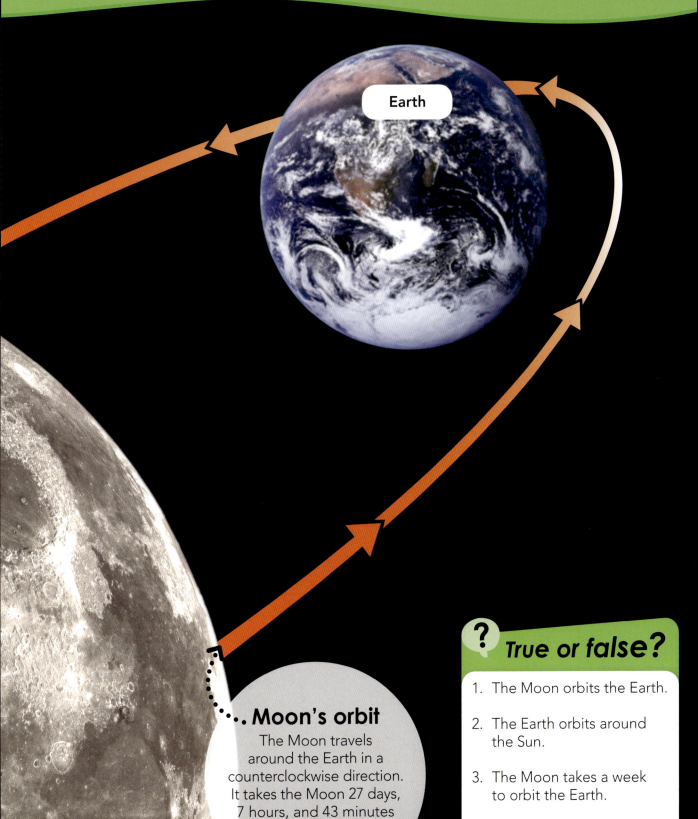

Earth

Moon's orbit
The Moon travels around the Earth in a counterclockwise direction. It takes the Moon 27 days, 7 hours, and 43 minutes to make one orbit.

❓ True or false?

1. The Moon orbits the Earth.

2. The Earth orbits around the Sun.

3. The Moon takes a week to orbit the Earth.

See pages 132–133 for the answers

Can you scream in space?

In space, nobody can hear you scream. This is because it is a vacuum—there is almost nothing there, including air like we have on Earth! Sound can't travel through a vacuum. When astronauts are inside a spacecraft, they can talk and hear sounds because there is air in the spacecraft.

Vacuum
A vacuum is an area with almost nothing in it, not even air! If there is a vacuum between an object making sound and your ear, you won't hear the sound.

How sound works
Sounds are vibrations that can travel through different materials. The vibrations make the air, or material around it vibrate and the vibrations then travel and enter your ears.

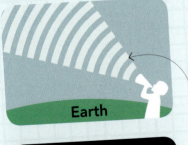

On the Earth we have air, so sound can travel.

There is no air on the Moon, so sound cannot travel.

What does it smell like in space?

The smell of space
Astronauts who have returned from space have struggled to describe the smell of their space suits after a space walk. Some say the space suits smell a bit burned and metallic, like the smell of hot metal.

Radio microphone
Spacewalking astronauts wear microphones so they can talk to each other by radio. Their space suits protect them from the vacuum of space.

? Quick quiz

1. Why do spacewalking astronauts wear microphones?

2. What is a vacuum?

3. Is there air in space?

See pages 132–133 for the answers

The solar system

This is where we live in the universe. The solar system is a collection of planets that travel around our closest star, the Sun.

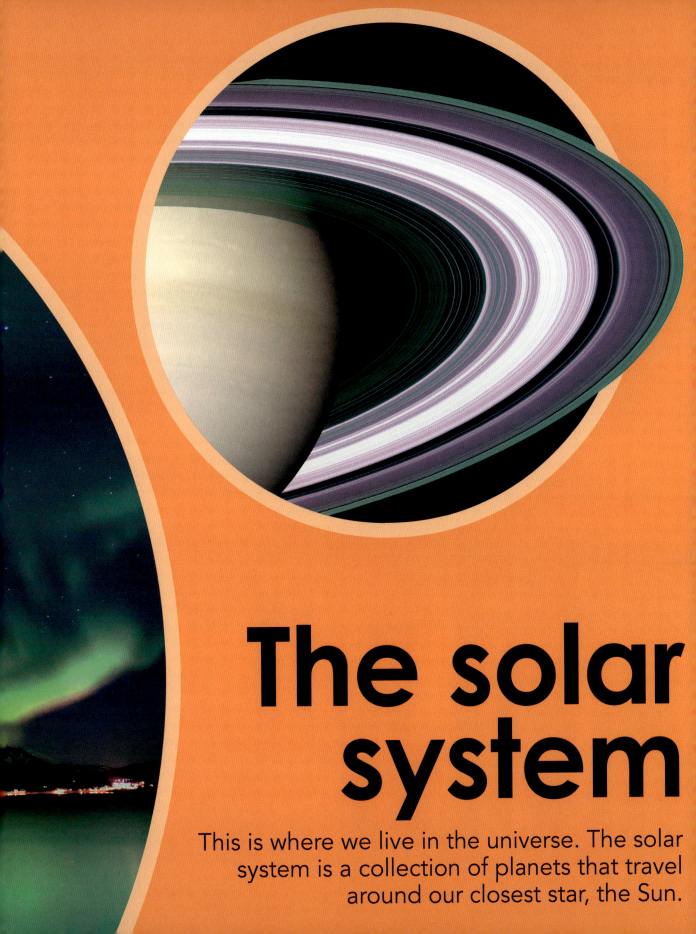

What is the solar system?

The solar system is our home in the universe. It is made up of our Sun at the center, with planets, dwarf planets, asteroids, and comets orbiting around it. Our solar system is just one of many similar systems in space.

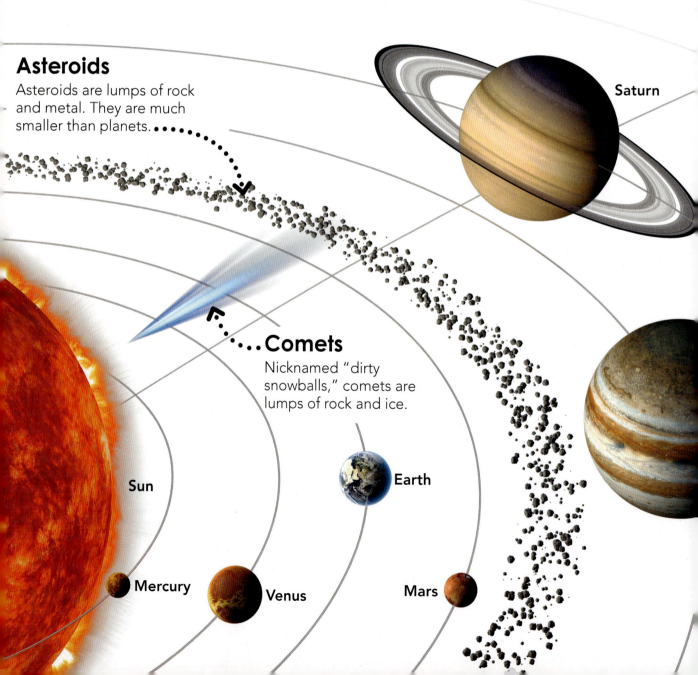

Asteroids
Asteroids are lumps of rock and metal. They are much smaller than planets.

Comets
Nicknamed "dirty snowballs," comets are lumps of rock and ice.

Saturn

Sun

Mercury

Venus

Earth

Mars

Where did the solar system come from?

The Sun
The solar system began 4.6 billion years ago when the Sun was formed. A cloud of gas and dust became squashed together by gravity. It began to draw more material toward it until it became the Sun.

Everything else
The bits of material left over after the sun formed clumped together into bigger and bigger pieces. These clumps became planets, dwarf planets, asteroids, comets, and moons.

Kuiper Belt
Toward the edge of the solar system is the Kuiper Belt. It is home to frozen objects, such as comets and dwarf planets.

Orbits
An orbit is the curved path that an object follows in space. The planets and everything else in our solar system orbit the Sun.

Pluto

Neptune

Uranus

Jupiter

Planets
There are eight planets in our solar system. Some planets are rocky, such as Earth and Mars, and others are made mostly of gas, such as Jupiter and Saturn.

? Quick quiz

1. Which planet is the biggest in our solar system?
   a) Jupiter
   b) Neptune
   c) Earth

2. Which planet is closest to the Sun?
   a) Venus
   b) Mercury
   c) Mars

See pages 132–133 for the answers

What are planets made of?

In our solar system, the four inner rocky planets—Mercury, Venus, Earth, and Mars—have solid surfaces that you could walk on. The surfaces of the two gas giants, Jupiter and Saturn, and the two ice giants, Uranus and Neptune, aren't solid, and you could not walk on them.

True or false?

1. There are eight rocky planets in the solar system.
2. Gas giants have a small, rocky core.
3. The surface of the Earth is called the crust.

See pages 132–133 for the answers

Crust
Rocky planets have a hard surface, which is known as the crust. Much of the Earth's crust is hidden by oceans.

Core
All rocky planets have a similar structure. Each has a metallic core, or center, which is mostly made of iron.

Mantle
The part of the planet between its crust and core is called the mantle. It is made of many rocky layers.

Mercury

What are planets outside our solar system made of?

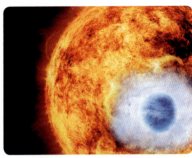

HD 189733b
Planets that orbit other stars are made of the same kind of stuff—rocks and gases—as the planets in our solar system. HD 189733b is a huge gas giant like Jupiter. It is blue and scientists think it possibly rains liquid glass!

Kepler 186f
This is the most "Earthlike" planet discovered so far. It is a similar size as our planet, and scientists think that, like Earth, it might be rocky and have water on its surface.

Scientists do not know the size of Jupiter's rocky core because it is hidden below layers of gas and liquid.

Layers
Unlike the rocky planets, ice and gas giants don't have a hard surface. They are made mostly of ice or gas with a small, rocky core.

Atmosphere
Ice and gas giants have many layers of clouds. Underneath the cloud tops, the atmosphere gets thicker and thicker.

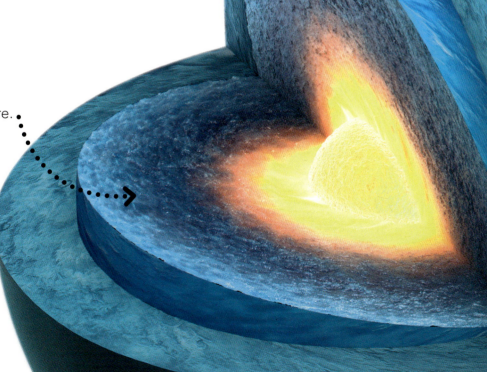

Uranus

Why is there life on Earth?

Earth is at just the right distance from the Sun for it to be not too hot and not too cold for life as we know it to exist. This is called the habitable zone. Our planet also has all the ingredients needed for life to begin and survive. These include liquid water, raw materials such as soil, and energy from the Sun.

Energy
For life to exist, there needs to be a constant source of energy. On Earth, that energy comes from the Sun.

? Picture quiz

What is the biggest animal on Earth?

See pages 132–133 for the answers

Raw materials
The raw materials that make up all living things can be found almost anywhere on Earth. Add water and energy to these materials and life can appear. This is how all plants, animals, and everything living on Earth began.

Where does life come from?

Stardust
All the ingredients that made the Earth and everything on it came from stardust. This was created when dying stars exploded. This means that we are all made from stardust! This dust later made more stars and planets like Earth.

Life began on Earth more than 3.5 billion years ago!

Water
Planet Earth has plenty of liquid water, unlike the other planets in our solar system. Water is essential for life—without it, life would not exist.

Why is Jupiter striped?

Jupiter is the biggest planet in the solar system. It has several stripes, or bands, of different colors. These bands are caused by chemicals in Jupiter's clouds and also by winds that whip around the planet, moving in different directions.

Rapid rotation
Jupiter is the fastest spinning planet in the solar system. It takes less than 10 hours to make one complete turn, or rotation.

Strong winds
Jupiter is a very windy and stormy planet. Its winds are created deep inside the planet and blow across it at hundreds of miles an hour.

Great Red Spot
The red spot on Jupiter is a huge spinning storm that has been raging for hundreds of years. It is the biggest storm in the solar system.

? Picture quiz

On which planet was this giant storm spotted?

See pages 132–133 for the answers

Icy clouds

Jupiter's north pole is covered in icy storm clouds. The pole also has massive light shows, which are similar to the auroras that are seen on Earth.

Which other planets are stormy?

Great White Spot
Huge thunderstorms raging on Saturn show up every few years as the Great White Spot. They often spread right around the planet.

Great Dark Spots
Neptune is the windiest planet in the solar system. It has giant dark spots, which are gigantic spinning storms, like hurricanes. These spots will often suddenly appear and then disappear again.

In 2010, one of Jupiter's big stripes disappeared. It then reappeared a few months later.

Is there life on Mars?

Long ago, Mars was probably warmer and wetter than it is now, with a thicker atmosphere, or layer of gas, surrounding the planet. This means that life as we know it could once have survived on Mars. There may even be tiny life forms there today.

What is the weather like on Mars?

Dust storms
Mars often has huge dust storms. These storms are sometimes so big that they can be seen by telescopes on Earth.

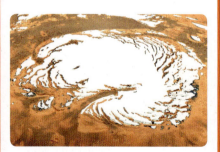

Cold weather
Mars is a cold world, with a much thinner atmosphere than Earth. Its average temperature is a chilly -76°F (-60°C).

Olympus Mons
The largest volcano in the solar system is on Mars. It is called Olympus Mons, and it is 16 miles (25 km) high, which is nearly three times the height of Mount Everest.

Frozen poles

Just like Earth, Mars has ice caps covering its north and south poles. The ice is made of frozen water and frozen carbon dioxide.

? True or false?

1. Mars is a smaller planet than Earth.

2. Mars does not have a south pole.

3. Mars may have once had life.

See pages 132–133 for the answers

Signs of water

The rule used by scientists who are looking for life elsewhere in the universe is to follow the water! Streaks on Mars's surface are thought to have been made by the flow of very salty water.

34 THE SOLAR SYSTEM

Many rings
Saturn has many different sized rings circling around it. The larger ones were all named after a letter of the alphabet, in the order that they were discovered.

What are Saturn's rings made of?

When you look at Saturn through a telescope, you can see beautiful rings circling the planet. They are made of icy rock and dust. No one knows for sure why Saturn has rings. They may be the remains of a moon that was destroyed or material left over from when Saturn formed.

Gaps in the rings
The dark areas are gaps in between Saturn's rings. The biggest gap is called the Cassini Division and is thought to have been made by Mimas, one of Saturn's moons. As Mimas orbits Saturn, its gravity pulls rocks out of the rings.

Close-up
There are billions of pieces of ice, rock, and dust in Saturn's rings. The rings are as wide as the gap between the Earth and the Moon.

Do any other planets have rings around them?

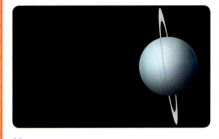

Uranus
Ice giant Uranus has rings that circle it. The rings are much smaller than those around Saturn. Uranus's neighbor Neptune has similar rings, too.

Jupiter
The rings that circle Jupiter are mostly made of dust. This dust was formed when space rocks, or meteoroids, crashed into some of Jupiter's moons.

? True or false?

1. Saturn is the only planet in the solar system with rings.

2. Saturn has more than one ring.

3. Jupiter has rings made of dust.

See pages 132–133 for the answers

Is Pluto a planet?

Pluto is a planet, but a particular type of one. It is a dwarf planet and is much smaller than other planets. Like other planets it orbits the Sun, but it does not have a clear orbital path—this means it has lots of neighbors in its path around the Sun.

Small and distant
Pluto is smaller than Earth's Moon. It is even smaller than North America! Pluto is far away from the Sun in a region of the solar system called the Kuiper Belt, which lies beyond the planet Neptune.

Pluto's heart
This part of Pluto's surface is shaped like a heart. It is smooth and doesn't have craters. Its name is Tombaugh Regio, after Clyde Tombaugh, the American astronomer who discovered Pluto in 1930.

Pluto's surface
There are craters, gigantic rivers of ice called glaciers, and mountains on Pluto's surface. Scientists think there may also be volcanoes that spew out ice instead of lava.

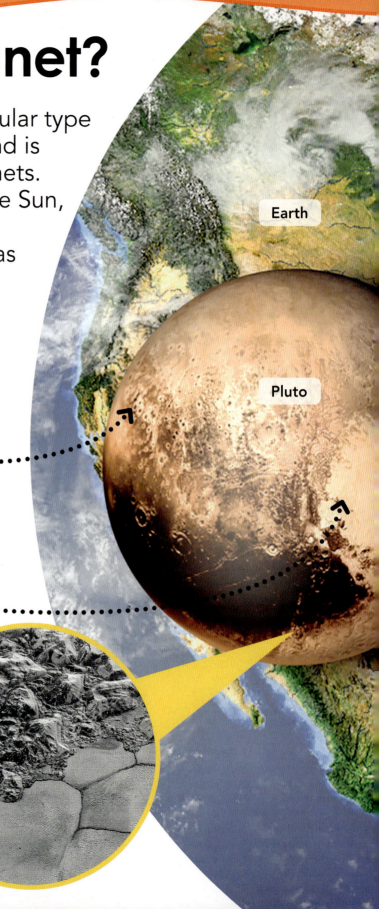

37

❓ Quick quiz

1. What is Pluto?

2. How many dwarf planets have been discovered so far?

3. Does Pluto have moons?

See pages 132–133 for the answers

Are there other dwarf planets?

Makemake
Makemake is a cold dwarf planet and it has at least one moon. So far, there are five known dwarf planets, and four of them are in the Kuiper Belt. There are probably many more waiting to be discovered.

Haumea
This dwarf planet takes 283 Earth years to complete one orbit around the Sun. Haumea is shaped like a football and has two moons. A space probe has not yet visited Haumea.

38 THE SOLAR SYSTEM

Corona
The second-hottest part of the Sun is its outer atmosphere (layer of gas), called the corona. Scientists do not yet understand why it is hotter than the surface.

Solar flare
Solar flares are gigantic eruptions of energy from the surface of the Sun. They can take days to build up before exploding in a dramatic fashion. They are the biggest explosive events in the solar system, and they can last from a few minutes to several hours.

How hot is the Sun?

The Sun is a sizzling ball of gas. It is our closest star and the hottest thing in our solar system. If you were able to stick a thermometer on its surface, it would read a scorching 11,000°F (6,000°C). The hottest part of the Sun, however, is its center, or core.

Which planets are the hottest?

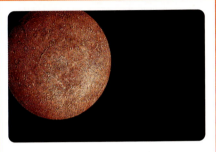

Mercury
Temperatures on tiny Mercury can reach a searing 790°F (420°C). It is the closest planet to the Sun.

Venus
Even though Venus is farther away from the Sun than Mercury, it is actually hotter. Venus has a thick atmosphere covered by clouds that trap in the Sun's heat.

Sunspots

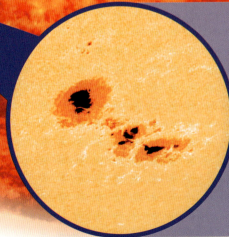

Sunspots are dark spots that appear on the Sun's surface. They are the coolest parts of the Sun and often appear in pairs.

? Quick quiz

1. Which is the hottest part of the Sun?

2. What are solar flares?

3. Can you guess how far away the Earth is from the Sun?

See pages 132–133 for the answers

Why does the Moon change its shape?

We can see the Moon in the day and night sky. Sometimes it is a bright, round circle, and other times it is a crescent shape. The Moon itself isn't really changing, it just looks different from Earth. This is because we see different amounts of the sunlit side of the Moon as it orbits Earth.

Phases of the Moon

The Moon takes just under 28 days to orbit the Earth. The different shapes that the Moon appears to be are called phases. This is what the Moon's orbit looks like from space.

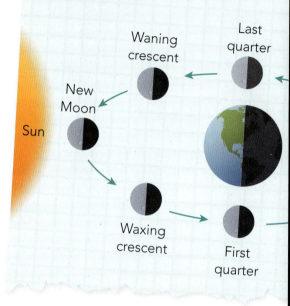

1. New Moon
In this phase, we cannot see the Moon from Earth because its lit face is directly toward the Sun.

2. Waxing crescent
As the Moon moves away from the Sun, we see sunlight reflected off a tiny part of it. We see a sliver, or crescent.

3. First quarter
The Moon has now traveled a quarter of its orbit. We can see about half of it.

4. Waxing gibbous
The Moon becomes bigger each night. It's described as "gibbous," which means it looks swollen on one side.

1

2

3

4

What are the two sides of the Moon?

Near side
The near side of the Moon is the side that always faces Earth. The Earth helps to shield it from collisions with space rocks, but some do still hit it and make craters.

Far side
The far side of the Moon never faces the Earth. The only people who have ever seen the far side are astronauts who have flown over it. There are many craters on this side.

The Moon is the brightest object that you can see in the night sky!

? True or false?

1. Earth orbits the Moon.
2. The far side of the Moon has many craters.
3. There are eight phases of the Moon.

See pages 132–133 for the answers

5. Full Moon
The entire part of the Moon facing the Earth now reflects the Sun's light.

6. Waning gibbous
The Moon is now waning, or shrinking. It will keep waning until there's another new Moon.

7. Last quarter
The Moon is now three-quarters of the way around the Earth.

8. Waning crescent
We can now see just a sliver of the Moon. It has almost completed a full orbit of the Earth.

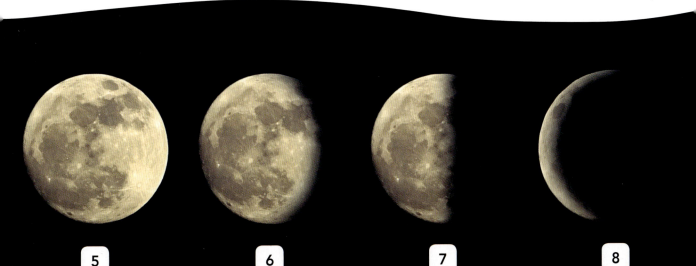

Can it be dark in the daytime?

A solar eclipse can cause it to be dark on Earth during the daytime. This is when the Moon passes directly between the Earth and the Sun. The Moon blocks out the sunlight, making some places on Earth become dark.

How a solar eclipse works

When the Moon reaches a certain point in its orbit, it sometimes passes directly between the Earth and the Sun. The Moon is smaller than the Sun, but, because it is closer to Earth, it can block out the Sun's light completely. Sometimes only part of the Sun is covered—this is called a partial eclipse.

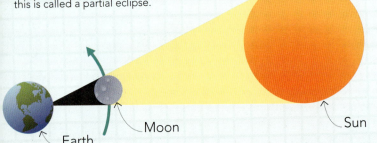

Earth — Moon — Sun

Are there other events similar to solar eclipses?

Lunar eclipse
A lunar eclipse is when the Earth passes between the Moon and the Sun. Earth's shadow makes the Moon go dark, but some sunlight reaches the Moon and causes it to appear red.

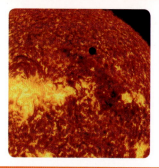

Venus transit
Sometimes Venus and Mercury pass between the Earth and the Sun. This is called a transit. The black dot here shows Venus crossing the Sun.

43

During a solar eclipse, birds might get confused and stop singing!

Sun's corona
When the Moon covers the Sun, the Sun's atmosphere can be seen. This is known as the "corona."

Diamond ring
Just at the point when the Moon covers the Sun, a beautiful flash of light can be seen. This is called the "Diamond Ring."

? Quick quiz

1. Can you guess how long a solar eclipse takes?

2. Why should people wear special glasses to watch a solar eclipse?

3. What is it called when the Moon only covers part of the Sun?

See pages 132–133 for the answers

Do other planets have moons?

Earth is not the only planet with a moon. Most other planets in our solar system have moons, except for Mercury and Venus. The dwarf planet Pluto has five moons and even some asteroids have moons.

Miranda
Tiny Miranda orbits Uranus. This moon looks like it is made of lots of different pieces that don't quite fit together. It is home to the largest cliff in the solar system.

Ganymede
This is the biggest moon in the solar system—even bigger than the planet Mercury! Ganymede is one of the many moons—there are over 70—that orbit Jupiter.

Could there be life on any moons?

Europa
This moon orbits Jupiter. It has a liquid ocean lurking beneath its frozen surface. Scientists think it is possible that there could be life in Europa's ocean.

Titan
This moon of Saturn is the only one in our solar system with an atmosphere. Scientists think Titan could be like a young Earth, and that some form of life may exist there.

Io

This moon of Jupiter is the most volcanic place in our solar system. Io has hundreds of active volcanoes. Some of them spew out plumes of lava that rise hundreds of miles high.

Enceladus

Saturn has over 80 moons, and Enceladus is the sixth largest. It is covered in an icy crust that has an ocean below it. Eruptions of rock and dust from Enceladus have formed one of Saturn's outer rings.

? Picture quiz

Which rocky, red planet do these two oddly shaped moons belong to?

See pages 132–133 for the answers

THE SOLAR SYSTEM

What would happen if a meteor hit the Earth?

Many pieces of space rock and dust enter the Earth's atmosphere every day, but most burn up before they reach the surface. Sometimes small pieces survive and hit the ground. Very rarely, large rocks hit the Earth, and they can make big craters, such as Barringer Crater in Arizona.

Meteoroid

Meteor

Meteorite

Viewing platform
This specially built viewing platform lets visitors peer down into the huge crater.

Meteoroids, meteors, and meteorites

Meteoroids, meteors, and meteorites are practically the same thing—the only difference is their location. A meteoroid is a piece of rock or metal that is moving through space. If it enters Earth's atmosphere, it is then a meteor. If it doesn't burn up and lands on the Earth, it is then a meteorite.

Earth's atmosphere

Earth

How can you find a meteorite?

Choose your location
Meteorites are easiest to spot in places that have few earth rocks. These places are deserts, dry lake beds, or on the frozen continent of Antarctica.

Use a metal detector
Some meteorites contain metal, such as iron and nickel, and so a metal detector can help you hunt for them!

Barringer Crater
Barringer Crater was named after Daniel Barringer. He was the first person to suggest that the crater was made by a meteorite that had hit the Earth.

Deep crater
This crater was made by a meteorite that crashed to Earth about 50,000 years ago. It is 560 ft (170 m) deep and 3,900 ft (1,200 m) wide.

? Quick quiz

1. Where would you find a meteoroid?
2. Where is Barringer Crater?
3. What is a meteorite?

See pages 132–133 for the answers

What is a shooting star?

A shooting star isn't really a star, it is a meteor. This is a piece of rock or dust from space that enters the Earth's atmosphere. As it moves through our atmosphere, it heats up and shines bright as it streaks through the sky. When there are lots of shooting stars, it is called a meteor shower.

Most meteor showers don't make a sound, but sometimes a hissing noise can be heard.

Burning up
The pieces of rock and dust are normally very small. They will usually burn up before they reach the Earth.

Bright streak
As the rock falls toward Earth at high speed, it becomes very hot. This makes the rock and the air around it glow as it speeds through the atmosphere.

What is a meteor shower?

Comets give off lots of pieces of rock and dust when they travel through space. When Earth's orbit takes it through this trail, the particles enter the Earth's atmosphere and create a meteor shower.

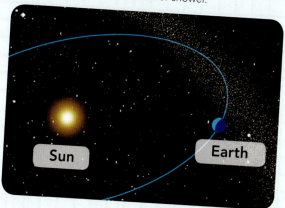

Earth passing through comet dust

Which are the best meteor showers to look out for?

Leonid meteor shower
The Leonids are caused by the comet Tempel-Tuttle. They can be seen every November, around the middle of the month.

Perseid meteor shower
This is one of the most popular meteor showers of the year. The Perseid meteor shower is known for its many fast and bright "shooting stars." It can be seen around the middle of August.

? True or false?

1. You can see the Perseid meteor shower in August.

2. Halley's Comet causes the Leonids.

3. A shooting star is a star falling to the Earth.

See pages 132–133 for the answers

Why do comets have tails?

Comets are made of gas, dust, and ice that was left over from when the solar system formed. Comets do not have tails all the time. When a comet passes close to the Sun, it heats up and spews out gasses and dust, which glow.

How comet tails form
Comets travel around the Sun in an oval-shaped path. As a comet passes close to the Sun, it starts throwing out dust and gas because the nucleus is heated by the Sun. This forms a tail that points away from the Sun.

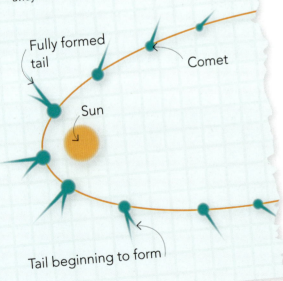

Comet's nucleus
The head of a comet is called the nucleus. It is often known as a "dirty snowball."

Coma
This cloud of dust and ice around the comet's nucleus is called the coma. This is where the tail starts to form as the "snowball" melts.

Comet's tail

The comet's dust tail streaks across the sky for many millions of miles. The tail always points away from the Sun.

Is it possible to land on a comet?

Philae

After a 10-year journey across our solar system, the *Rosetta* spacecraft successfully sent a lander, called *Philae*, onto the surface of a comet in 2014.

❓ True or false?

1. Comets always have tails.

2. The head of a comet is sometimes known as a "dirty snowball."

3. A lander called *Rosetta* has visited the surface of a comet.

See pages 132–133 for the answers

What is the asteroid belt?

The asteroid belt is a ring of big rocks, called asteroids, that orbit the sun. It is found between the planets Mars and Jupiter. There are hundreds of thousands of asteroids in the belt, and they come in many different shapes and sizes.

Trojans
These asteroids travel around the sun in the same orbit as Jupiter. They travel in two groups—one group ahead of Jupiter and the other trailing behind it.

Dividing belt
The asteroid belt separates the four inner, rocky planets from Jupiter and the other outer planets.

What can we learn from asteroids?

Vesta
Asteroids, such as Vesta, were left over from when the solar system formed billions of years ago. Studying asteroids can help scientists understand how planets, such as the Earth, were formed.

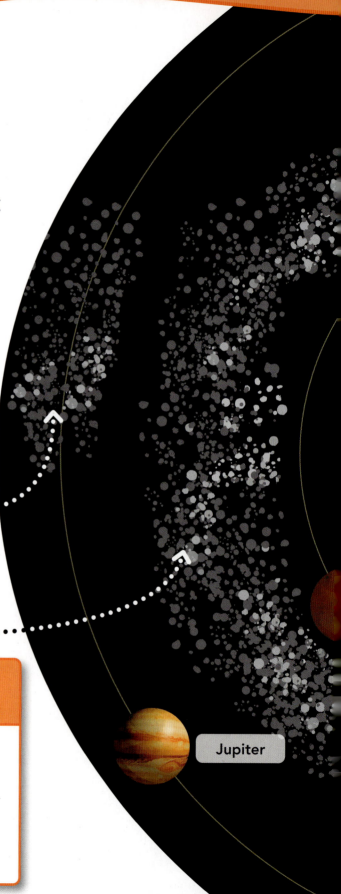

Jupiter

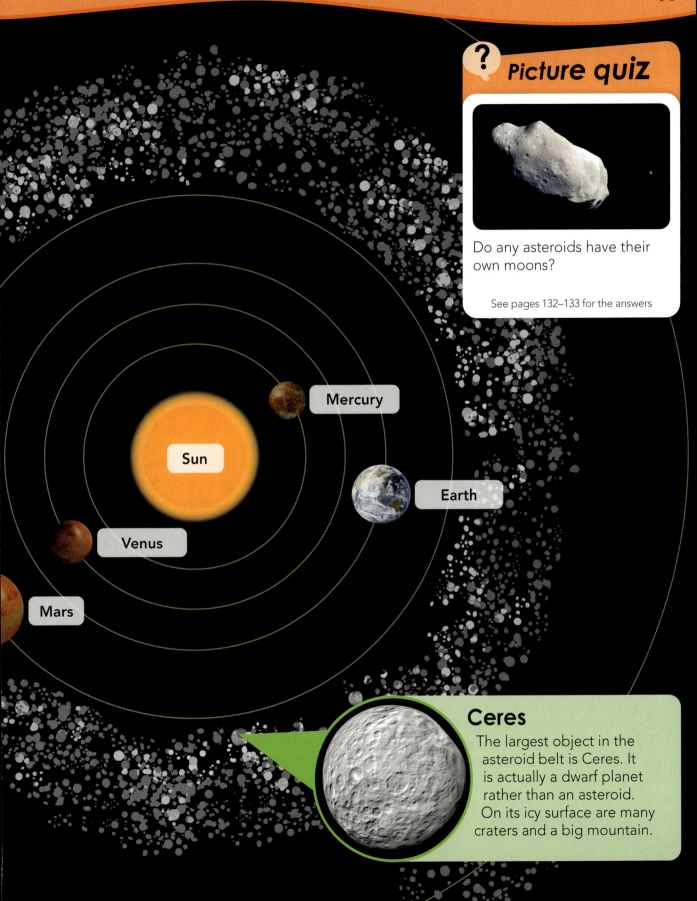

Picture quiz

Do any asteroids have their own moons?

See pages 132–133 for the answers

Ceres
The largest object in the asteroid belt is Ceres. It is actually a dwarf planet rather than an asteroid. On its icy surface are many craters and a big mountain.

THE SOLAR SYSTEM

Can you see the Earth from other planets?

Sometimes when you look up at the night sky, you can see some of the other planets in the solar system. If you could visit these planets, you'd be able to see the Earth in a similar way.

Saturn
In the corner of this picture is the planet Saturn. It looks dark because the Sun is behind it.

Cassini–Huygens
This photograph was taken by the *Cassini* spacecraft. *Cassini* and its companion spacecraft, *Huygens*, visited Saturn to help us learn more about the planet and its largest moon, Titan.

What does the Earth look like from space?

Paris at night
Astronauts living in space and orbiting the Earth can see whole cities from above. The bright lights of Paris look like a beautiful painting in this photograph taken from the International Space Station (ISS).

Erupting volcano
Volcanoes erupting plumes of smoke and ash can be seen from space. The astronauts in the ISS were the first to see the eruption of this volcano, called Mount Cleveland, in Alaska.

A tiny dot
This pale blue dot is the Earth. It is 746 million miles from Saturn. In the future, people may travel far enough into space to see the Earth looking just like this.

True or false?

1. You can see the Earth from other planets.

2. You can't see volcanoes from space.

3. From far away, the Earth looks like a pale blue dot.

See pages 132–133 for the answers

What are auroras?

Auroras are naturally occurring light displays that can be seen near the north and south poles. Auroras are formed when particles from the Sun enter the Earth's atmosphere at high speed and hit the gases there. This creates colorful curtains of light that appear to float in the sky.

Are there auroras on other planets?

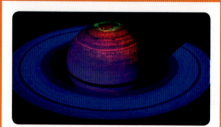

Saturn
Auroras sometimes appear at Saturn's north and south poles. This false-color image shows a dazzling green aurora display around the gas giant's south pole.

Jupiter
Auroras on Jupiter are the most incredible in the whole solar system. This aurora over Jupiter's north pole covers an area bigger than planet Earth!

Different patterns
Auroras paint amazingly beautiful patterns in the sky. Sometimes the patterns are swirly or shaped like spirals.

Different colors
You can spot a lot of different colors during an aurora display. The most common color is green, but you may also see purple, pink, red, and yellow.

Astronauts in space can sometimes see auroras as they orbit the Earth.

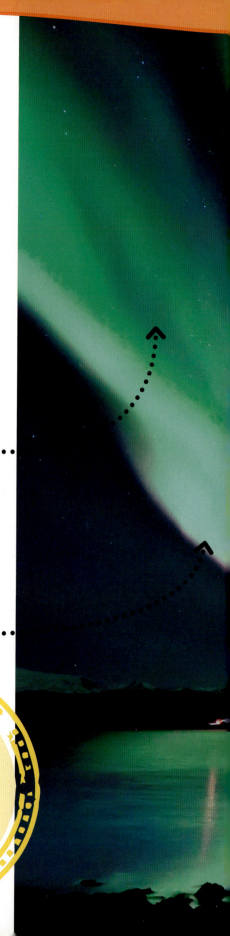

True or false?

1. The best places to see auroras on Earth are near the north and south poles.

2. Auroras can include a lot of different colors.

3. Jupiter has the biggest aurora in the solar system.

See pages 132–133 for the answers

Could you live on Venus?

Venus is roughly the same size and shape as Earth, but you wouldn't want to live there. It has a thick, toxic atmosphere and temperatures can get as hot as 880°F (471°C). If an unprotected spacecraft landed on the surface of Venus, it would begin to melt in minutes!

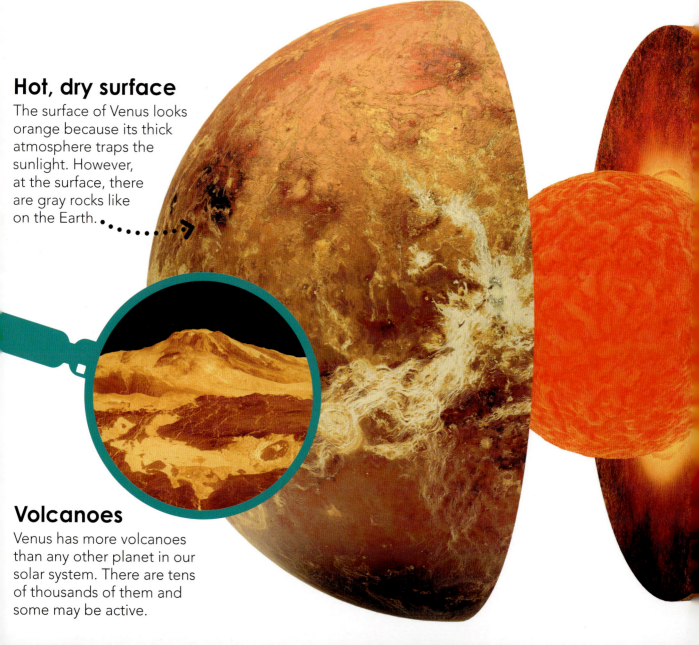

Hot, dry surface
The surface of Venus looks orange because its thick atmosphere traps the sunlight. However, at the surface, there are gray rocks like on the Earth.

Volcanoes
Venus has more volcanoes than any other planet in our solar system. There are tens of thousands of them and some may be active.

Thick clouds

Venus has a thick layer of clouds that are made of droplets of acid. These dangerous clouds speed around the planet, driven by hurricane-force winds.

Toxic air

Venus's atmosphere is made of toxic carbon dioxide gas. It traps in heat, making the planet very hot. There is no oxygen for humans to breathe on Venus.

How do we know what Venus is like?

Mariner 2
The first spacecraft to fly around Venus was NASA's *Mariner 2* in 1962. Since then, many spacecraft have been to Venus.

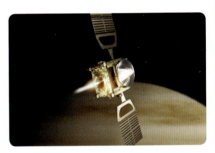

Venus Express
Venus Express was a spacecraft that was sent to learn more about Venus's atmosphere. It was launched in 2005.

? True or false?

1. Venus is the closest planet to the Sun.

2. Venus has lots of volcanoes.

3. Venus is covered in lots of orange rocks.

See pages 132–133 for the answers

Beyond Earth's orbit

Deep space is the universe beyond our Earth. Many amazing planets, stars, and galaxies are made and can be found there.

How many stars are there in the universe?

From Earth, we can see thousands of stars in the night sky, but there are many more farther out in space. In fact, there are more stars in the universe than grains of sand on all the beaches and deserts on Earth.

What is the closest star to our Sun?

Proxima Centauri
The closest star to our Sun is called Proxima Centauri. It is very far away from the Sun and from Earth—so far that light from it takes more than four years to reach us on Earth.

Scientists think there are about 1,000 billion trillion stars in the universe!

Counting stars
To figure out the number of stars in the universe, scientists multiply the number of stars in a galaxy by the number of galaxies they think there are.

? Picture quiz

Most stars live together in galaxies. Can you guess what type of galaxy this is?

See pages 132–133 for the answers

Young stars
This picture was taken by the Hubble Space Telescope. It shows a place in space where stars are formed.

Where do stars come from?

Stars are big balls of gas that give off heat and light. They begin their lives in huge clouds of gas and dust that are called nebulas. There are many different nebulas scattered throughout most galaxies.

How stars are born
New stars are being born every day and they all go through the same growing process. The Sun was created in this way 4.6 billion years ago.

Clumps of gas form
Inside a nebula, clumps of gas start to come together inside a molecular cloud.

The clumps contract
These clumps of gas and dust contract, or become smaller. The gravity of this new clump pulls in more dust from around it.

A spinning disk
The clump shrinks to form a hot, dense core. It is surrounded by a spinning disk of matter with jets of gas that shoot out from the top and bottom.

The star lights up
When the center is hot enough, energy is released and a star is born. A disk of extra matter still orbits the young star.

The disk moves on
The leftover disk material can become planets, moons, asteroids, or comets—or may just remain as dust.

Eagle Nebula
The Eagle Nebula is a region of gas and dust in space where stars form. It is more than 5.5 million years old!

Have other nebulas been discovered?

Horsehead Nebula
The Horsehead Nebula was discovered by astronomers in 1888. It makes a beautiful picture in space.

Carina Nebula
The Carina Nebula is about 7,500 light-years from the Earth. It is thought to be home to more than 14,000 stars!

Pillars of Creation
These columns of gas and dust are called the Pillars of Creation, because stars are born inside them. They are about 57 trillion miles (92 trillion km) high. That is twice the distance from the Sun to the closest star.

? True or false?

1. Stars form in clouds of gas and dust.

2. The Sun is six billion years old.

See pages 132–133 for the answers

BEYOND EARTH'S ORBIT

Are all stars the same?

Stars come in lots of different sizes and colors. Some are gigantic, many times bigger than the Sun. Other stars are tiny and not very bright. Here are some of the types of star that have been discovered in the universe so far.

Most stars that you can see in the night sky without a telescope are bigger than the Sun.

Red supergiant

These stars are huge! If you were to put the Sun next to a red supergiant you would hardly be able to see it. These massives stars were once smaller, and are now closer to the end of their life cycle.

Blue supergiant

In space, the hottest stars are blue. Blue supergiants are extremely hot and bright, but are smaller in size than the red supergiants.

Are there stars that are smaller than the Sun?

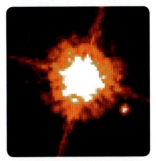

Red dwarf
Stars that are small are known as dwarf stars. A red dwarf is a star that is much smaller and cooler than the Sun.

White dwarf
A white dwarf is what is left over from a star like our Sun, when it has come to the end of its life. It is very heavy and small, about the same size as the Earth.

Blue giant

Large and compact, blue giants burn fuel quickly. This means they reach really high temperatures and are very bright.

The sun

The Sun is an average star, also known as a main sequence star. There are many stars similar to our Sun in the universe.

Orange subgiant

Between a red giant and a star like the Sun, is the orange subgiant. Our Sun will turn into an orange subgiant toward the end of its life, before it becomes a red giant.

Red giant

Red giants are stars that are near the end of their life. They are much cooler and larger than the Sun.

? True or false?

1. Some stars are giants.
2. Some stars are dwarfs.
3. Our Sun is a giant star.

See pages 132–133 for the answers

What is a light-year?

A light-year is the distance light is able to travel in a year. In space, things are very far apart, so astronomers use light-years to measure how far away things are from each other. In one year, light can travel nearly 6.2 trillion miles (10 trillion km).

Closest neighbor
The Andromeda Galaxy is the nearest galaxy to the Milky Way. It is roughly 2.5 million light years away from us.

Speed of light
In one second, light can travel 186,500 miles (300,000 km) through space. This means light from the Sun takes more than eight minutes to reach the Earth.

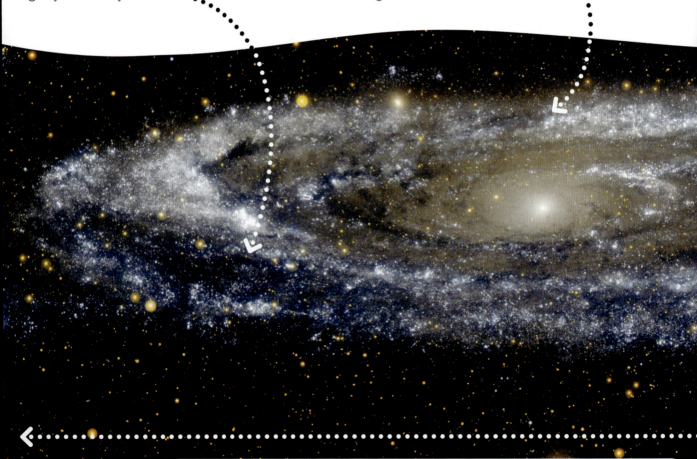

The Andromeda Galaxy is 260,000 light-years across. The Milky Way is smaller at about 140,000 light-years across.

How fast can we travel in space?

A fast orbit
The International Space Station orbits the Earth at a speed of around 17,200 mph (28,000 kph). At this speed it travels around the Earth once every 90 minutes.

Speedy spacecraft
The NASA spacecraft *Juno* reached a top speed of about 165,000 mph (265,000 kph) as it arrived at the planet Jupiter in 2016.

Andromeda
The Andromeda galaxy has trillions of stars, which is more than the Milky Way. Light from Andromeda's stars takes 2.5 million years to reach us on the Earth.

Nothing on Earth or in space can travel faster than the speed of light.

? Quick quiz

1. What is the speed of light?

2. How long does it take light from the Sun to reach the Earth?

3. How long does it take the International Space Station to orbit the Earth?

See pages 132–133 for the answers

What is a black hole?

Black holes are among the most mysterious and incredible things in the universe. They aren't real holes, but are areas where matter has been squashed into a tiny space.

Keep your distance!
Don't get too close to a black hole or you'll be swallowed up! The pulling force, or gravity, of a black hole is so powerful that nothing can escape it.

Invisible
Black holes are invisible to the human eye because no light can escape from them. Scientists use telescopes with special tools to find them.

What else can black holes do?

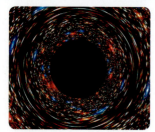

Bend space and light
The gravity of a black hole is so strong that it bends the space around it. Light passing near a black hole follows a curved path and eventually enters it.

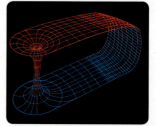

Stretch time
Black holes can stretch time! The closer you get to a black hole, the slower time goes. Some scientists even think black holes bend the shape of the universe and make shortcuts, called wormholes, between different parts of it.

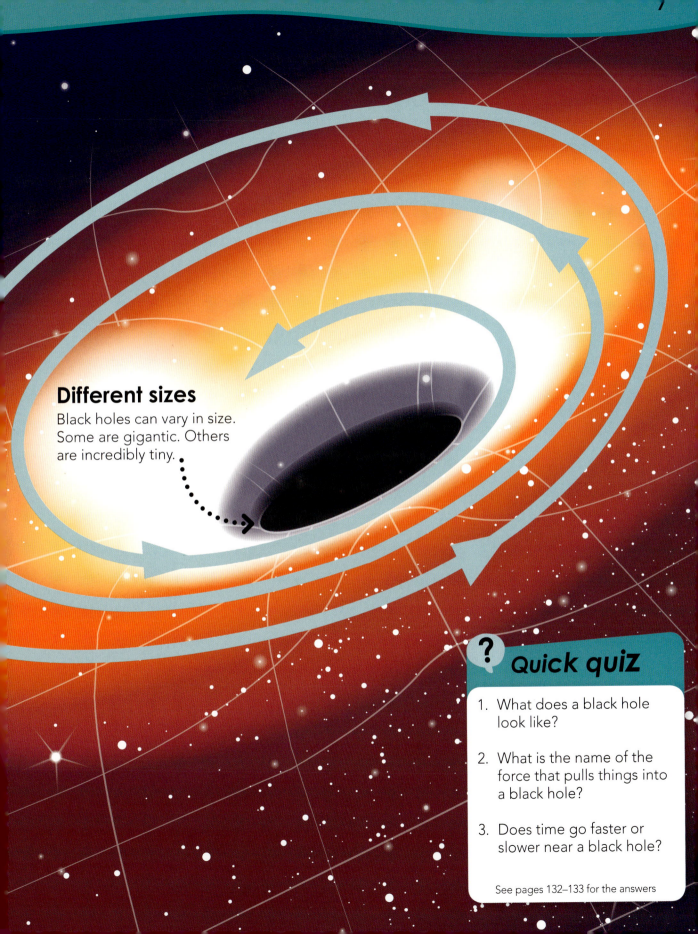

Different sizes

Black holes can vary in size. Some are gigantic. Others are incredibly tiny.

❓ Quick quiz

1. What does a black hole look like?

2. What is the name of the force that pulls things into a black hole?

3. Does time go faster or slower near a black hole?

See pages 132–133 for the answers

BEYOND EARTH'S ORBIT

Average star
An average star is a star like our Sun. This kind of star stays the same size and shape for about 10 billion years before it begins to die.

Red giant
As an average star nears the end of its life, it slowly begins to get bigger and cooler. It is then known as a red giant.

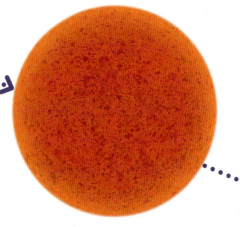

Stellar nursery
A stellar nursery, or nebula, is a cloud of very hot gas. Here, new stars are born. Stars are made from gas and dust. Stars with more gas and dust will be larger.

Massive star
Massive stars are formed in the same way as average stars. However, they are much bigger and use up energy faster, so they don't live as long.

Red supergiant
This is the largest type of star in the universe. Red supergiants are massive stars that have become bigger and cooler toward the end of their life.

What happens when stars die?

Just like everything else in our universe, stars are born and eventually die. Some stars have very quiet deaths, and others end with massive explosions. Follow this diagram to see how different stars change throughout their lives.

Planetary nebula

As the star starts to run out of fuel, its core, or center, collapses and it loses its outer layers. It is now known as a planetary nebula.

White dwarf

The leftover core of the star is called a white dwarf. This will eventually cool to become a black dwarf.

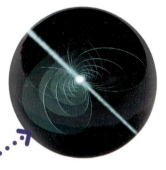

Neutron star

These are tightly packed, tiny stars. They measure no more than 10 miles (16 km) across.

Supernova

At the end of the red supergiant's life, there is a massive explosion called a supernova. This throws the outer layers of the star out into space. The core of the star may become a neutron star or a black hole.

Black hole

A black hole forms when the core of a dying star becomes so tightly packed into a tiny space that nothing can escape—not even light.

When did we last see a supernova in the Milky Way?

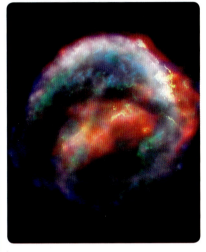

Kepler's Supernova
The last time we saw a supernova in our galaxy was just over 400 years ago. The explosion, now called Kepler's Supernova, was brighter than any other star in the night sky for a few weeks.

? Quick quiz

1. What does an average star become when it dies?
   a) A supernova
   b) A black hole
   c) A white dwarf

2. What is the biggest type of star?
   a) White dwarf
   b) Average star
   c) Red supergiant

See pages 132–133 for the answers

What shape is the Milky Way?

Our solar system is in the Milky Way galaxy. Galaxies, like planets and stars, are constantly spinning through space and hold many solar systems within them. The Milky Way is a spiral galaxy with arms that are made of clumps of stars.

There are around 200 billion galaxies in the known universe.

What other galaxy shapes are there?

Elliptical
Elliptical galaxies are egg-shaped and have no arms. The smallest and largest galaxies in the universe are elliptical. This elliptical galaxy, called M87, was discovered in the year 1781.

Irregular
Galaxies with no particular shape are called irregular galaxies. The galaxy shown here, called NGC 1569, is one example. They come in a range of different shapes and sizes.

Bright arms
The arms shine brightly because they are full of very bright young stars.

Dust clouds
As well as stars, galaxies are made up of huge quantities of dust and gas.

Milky Way
Viewed from the side, the Milky Way looks bar-shaped.

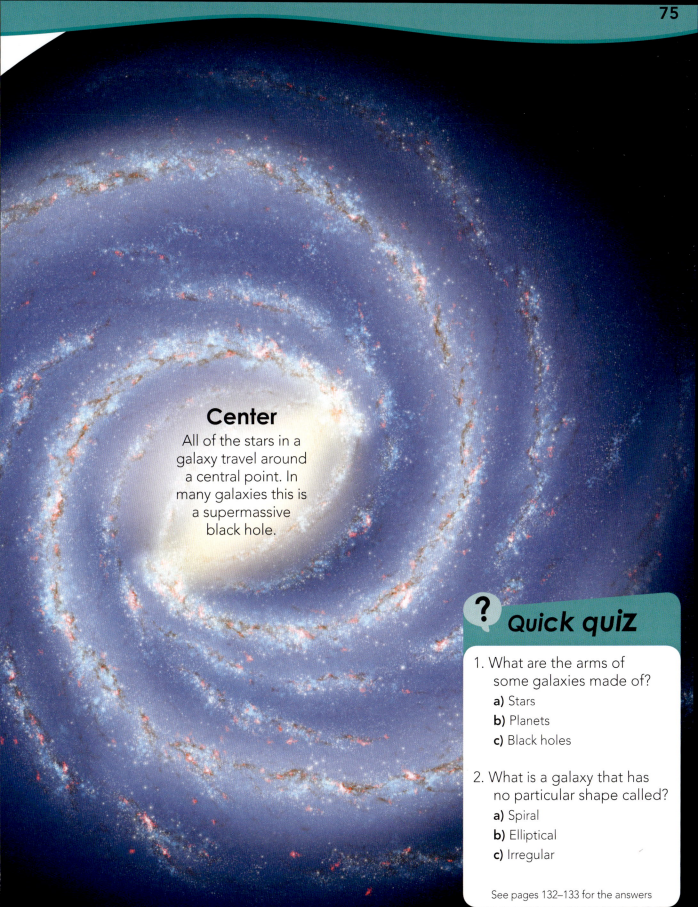

Center
All of the stars in a galaxy travel around a central point. In many galaxies this is a supermassive black hole.

? Quick quiz

1. What are the arms of some galaxies made of?
   a) Stars
   b) Planets
   c) Black holes

2. What is a galaxy that has no particular shape called?
   a) Spiral
   b) Elliptical
   c) Irregular

See pages 132–133 for the answers

Why do stars twinkle?

On a clear, dark night, you can see hundreds of stars shining in the sky. But stars don't actually twinkle, they only appear to do so because we are viewing them through the thick layers of the Earth's atmosphere.

Twinkle, twinkle little star

Stars are so far away from the Earth that they appear as tiny points of light in the sky. The light from the stars gets distorted as it travels through the Earth's atmosphere. This means that it doesn't travel in a straight line. The changing direction of the light makes the stars appear to twinkle!

Star patterns

Collections of stars in the night sky make shapes and patterns. Many are called constellations. This constellation is called Orion, the hunter. Orion is easy to spot because of the three stars in the middle that make up his belt.

What else can you see in the night sky?

Planet spotting
Planets in the night sky are generally brighter than stars and they don't twinkle. This image shows Venus and Mars.

The Moon
The Moon is the brightest object you can see in the night sky. If you look closely, you can see the dark plains on its surface.

? Quick quiz

1. Can you see planets in the night sky?

2. What are patterns of stars called?

3. What is the brightest object you can see in the night sky?

See pages 132–133 for the answers

Are there any planets outside our solar system?

When you look up at the night sky, most of the stars you can see probably have at least one planet orbiting around them. There are many planets outside our solar system and more are being discovered all the time.

What are rogue planets?

CFBDSIR 2149-0403
Some planets travel alone through space and do not orbit a parent star. These types of planets, such as CFBDSIR 2149-0403 pictured below, are known as rogue planets.

Planets that orbit around other stars are called exoplanets.

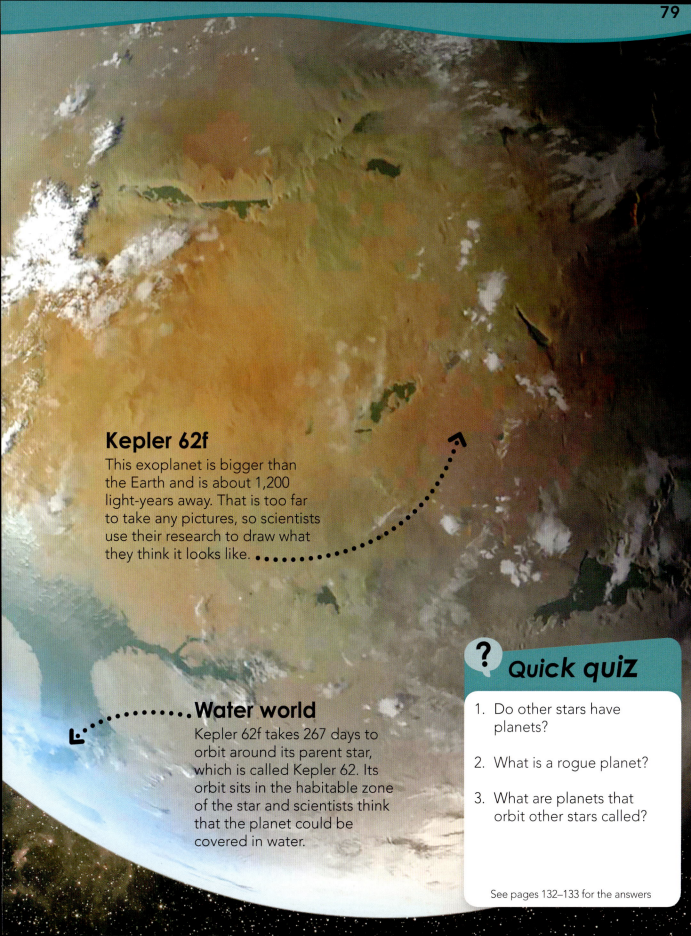

Kepler 62f
This exoplanet is bigger than the Earth and is about 1,200 light-years away. That is too far to take any pictures, so scientists use their research to draw what they think it looks like.

Water world
Kepler 62f takes 267 days to orbit around its parent star, which is called Kepler 62. Its orbit sits in the habitable zone of the star and scientists think that the planet could be covered in water.

Quick quiz

1. Do other stars have planets?

2. What is a rogue planet?

3. What are planets that orbit other stars called?

See pages 132–133 for the answers

What shines the brightest in the universe?

Quasars are the brightest objects in the universe. They are powered by huge black holes, called supermassive black holes, where stars, gas, and dust are being pulled inward. Some quasars can shine hundreds of times brighter than the whole of the Milky Way.

Beaming jets
Quasars give off huge amounts of energy. Jets of material burst outward as matter is ejected.

Far, far away
Quasars exist at the centers of distant galaxies. Even though they are extremely bright, they cannot be seen without powerful telescopes because they are so far away.

What do quasars look like through telescopes?

3C 273
Photographed by the Hubble Space Telescope, light from this quasar takes more than 2.5 billion years to reach the Earth. This was the first quasar to ever be discovered.

Colliding quasars
A pair of blue quasars in space were photographed crashing into each other more than 4.6 billion light-years away from the Earth.

Quasars are some of the farthest objects in the universe that are easy to see because they are so bright!

Black hole
A huge black hole is at the center of a quasar. It can be billions of times bigger than the Sun. One quasar has been discovered with two black holes at its center!

Accretion disk
This is a disk of material that is slowly being sucked into the black hole.

? True or false?

1. There is a black hole at the center of a quasar.
2. Quasars aren't very bright.
3. Quasars give off huge amounts of energy.

See pages 132–133 for the answers

Space exploration

People have been fascinated with space for thousands of years. New machines are always being invented to help us travel farther and learn more about the universe.

SPACE EXPLORATION

Laser beams

The Earth's atmosphere can make images from space look blurry. This telescope shoots a powerful laser beam into space to help correct the blurriness of the images caused by the atmosphere.

How do we look into space?

We can use devices called telescopes to look into space. They can be used to look closely at planets and the Moon and to find distant stars and galaxies. There are lots of telescopes on the Earth and there are also telescopes that orbit our planet.

How telescopes work

One of the most common types of telescope is a reflecting telescope. Light from an object, such as the Moon, enters through the top of the telescope and reflects, or bounces, off several angled mirrors. This creates a more detailed image than can be seen with the naked eye.

Light rays from the object enter the telescope.

Secondary mirror

Eyepiece

Main mirror

85

When was the telescope invented?

Galileo Galilei
In 1609, the Italian astronomer Galileo Galilei built his own telescope. It was an improved version of Hans Lippershey's invention. Galileo used it to make lots of discoveries, such as mountains and valleys on the surface of the Moon.

? Quick quiz

1. What is a telescope?
2. When did Galileo Galilei make his telescope?
3. How wide is the mirror on the Yepun telescope?

See pages 132–133 for the answers

Yepun telescope
The Yepun telescope is one of four large telescopes in Chile, South America. Its main mirror is 26 ft (8 m) wide—as wide as a tennis court! These four telescopes are used to see far into space.

Who were the first space explorers?

Early space explorers were the first people to ride in rockets, see the Earth from hundreds of miles away, and feel weightless. They were the pioneers of space travel.

Yuri Gagarin

The first person to travel in space was Yuri Gagarin. On April 12, 1961, the Russian orbited the Earth in his spacecraft *Vostok 1* for one hour and 48 minutes.

First man in space

First woman in space

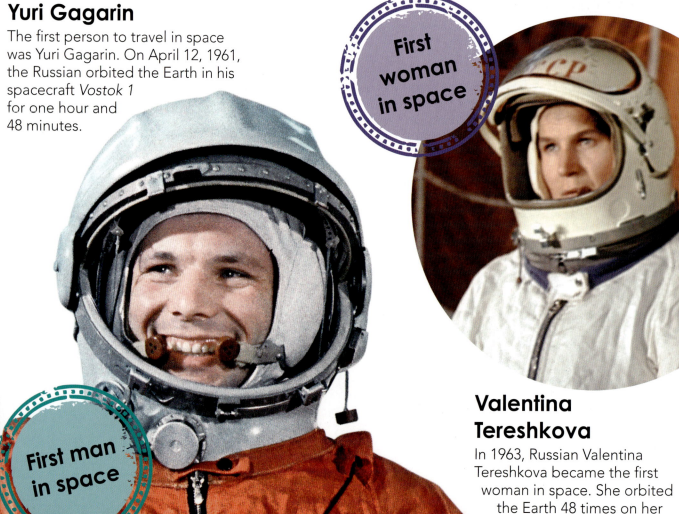

Valentina Tereshkova

In 1963, Russian Valentina Tereshkova became the first woman in space. She orbited the Earth 48 times on her three-day trip.

Apollo 8 crew

Americans Jim Lovell, Bill Anders, and Frank Borman were the first to leave the Earth's orbit. They circled the Moon in their 1968 mission.

First to leave the Earth's orbit

Apollo 11 crew

In 1969, Americans Neil Armstrong and Buzz Aldrin became the first people to walk on the Moon. Michael Collins accompanied them on their mission, but stayed in the spacecraft.

First people on the Moon

Alexey Leonov

In 1965, Russian Alexey Leonov was the first person to leave a spacecraft and take a "space walk." He floated in space for 12 minutes while attached to the spacecraft.

First walk in space

? Picture quiz

John Glenn went into space twice—first in 1962 and again in 1998. Can you guess which record he broke?

See pages 132–133 for the answers

Have animals been to space?

It's not just people who have explored space—animals were sent there first! They helped us understand about the effects of space travel on living things.

In 2007, tiny animals called tardigrades survived for 10 days in space outside a spacecraft!

Fruit flies
The first animals to travel into space were fruit flies in 1947. Scientists wanted to discover if space would harm the flies.

Mouse
In 1950, American scientists sent a mouse into space. They wanted to understand more about how living creatures cope in space.

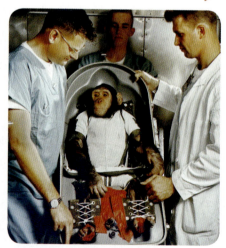

Chimpanzee
A chimpanzee named Ham was four years old when he was blasted into space in 1961. He spent 16 minutes there before his reentry capsule splashed back down in the Atlantic Ocean.

Dogs
In 1966, Russian scientists sent two dogs, called Veterok (left) and Ugolyok, into space together. The dogs orbited the Earth in their spacecraft *Cosmos 110* for 22 days, before returning safely.

Spiders
Two spiders, Anita and Arabella, were taken into space in 1973 to see if they could still make webs. The spiders soon got used to being weightless and spun their webs.

Laika

One of the most famous animal space explorers was a Russian dog called Laika. In 1957, she became the first animal to orbit the Earth. Her journey paved the way for human spaceflight.

? Quick quiz

1. What was the name of the first dog in space?

2. What were the first animals in space?

3. How old was Ham the chimpanzee when he went into space?

See pages 132–133 for the answers

90 SPACE EXPLORATION

November 3, 1957
Laika the Space Dog
Soviet space dog, Laika, was a stray that was found wandering the streets of Moscow. She traveled to space in the *Sputnik 2* spacecraft and became the first living creature to orbit the Earth.

April 9, 1959
Mercury 7
In response to the Soviet Union, the United States announced its first group of astronauts. Nicknamed "The Mercury 7," they were the best test pilots in the US.

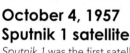

October 4, 1957
Sputnik 1 satellite
Sputnik 1 was the first satellite to be sent into space. Made by the Soviet Union, *Sputnik 1* orbited the Earth for three months.

The race starts here! 3... 2... 1... GO!

What was the Space Race?

The Space Race was a contest to conquer space between the United States and the Soviet Union - what we call Russia today. The race meant that humans began eagerly exploring space. It ended when the first astronaut walked on the Moon.

❓ Picture quiz

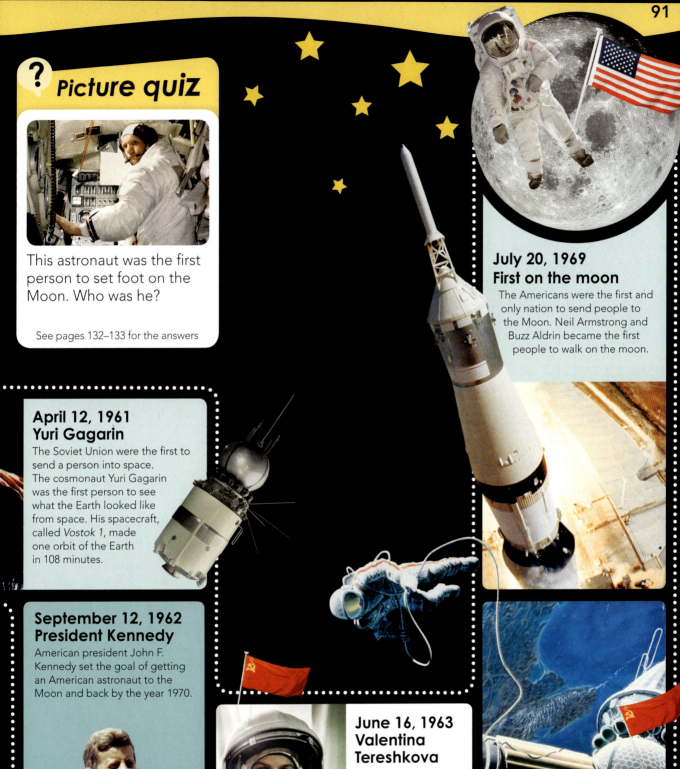

This astronaut was the first person to set foot on the Moon. Who was he?

See pages 132–133 for the answers

April 12, 1961
Yuri Gagarin
The Soviet Union were the first to send a person into space. The cosmonaut Yuri Gagarin was the first person to see what the Earth looked like from space. His spacecraft, called *Vostok 1*, made one orbit of the Earth in 108 minutes.

September 12, 1962
President Kennedy
American president John F. Kennedy set the goal of getting an American astronaut to the Moon and back by the year 1970.

July 20, 1969
First on the moon
The Americans were the first and only nation to send people to the Moon. Neil Armstrong and Buzz Aldrin became the first people to walk on the moon.

June 16, 1963
Valentina Tereshkova
Soviet cosmonaut Valentina Tereshkova became the first woman in space. She enjoyed skydiving and worked in a factory before training to be a cosmonaut.

March 18, 1965
First space walk
Cosmonaut Alexey Leonov became the first person to take a space walk outside a spacecraft—another success for the Soviet Union.

How many people have been to the Moon?

Only 12 people have walked on the Moon. They were all American astronauts and made their trips between 1969 and 1972. As there is no air on the Moon, the astronauts had to wear special space suits with an air supply for them to breathe.

Buzz Aldrin
After Neil Armstrong, Buzz Aldrin was the next person to set foot on the Moon. He collected rock samples and set up experiments.

The moonwalkers
These are the astronauts who have had the amazing experience of walking on the Moon. They landed on the Moon in six separate Apollo missions.

Neil Armstrong
Apollo 11

Buzz Aldrin
Apollo 11

Pete Conrad
Apollo 12

Alan Bean
Apollo 12

Alan Shepard
Apollo 14

Edgar Mitchell
Apollo 14

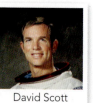
David Scott
Apollo 15

James Irwin
Apollo 15

John Young
Apollo 16

Charles Duke
Apollo 16

Eugene Cernan
Apollo 17

Harrison Schmitt
Apollo 17

Neil Armstrong

This photo was taken by Neil Armstrong, the first person to set foot on the Moon. You can see his reflection in Buzz Aldrin's visor.

What did astronauts do on the Moon?

Drove a rover

Some astronauts drove a special car on the Moon called a lunar rover. They used the rover to explore the Moon.

Science experiments

Astronauts did lots of experiments on the Moon to help scientists understand more about how the Moon was formed.

? Quick quiz

1. How many people have walked on the Moon?

2. Who was the last person to walk on the Moon?

3. Is there air on the Moon?

See pages 132–133 for the answers

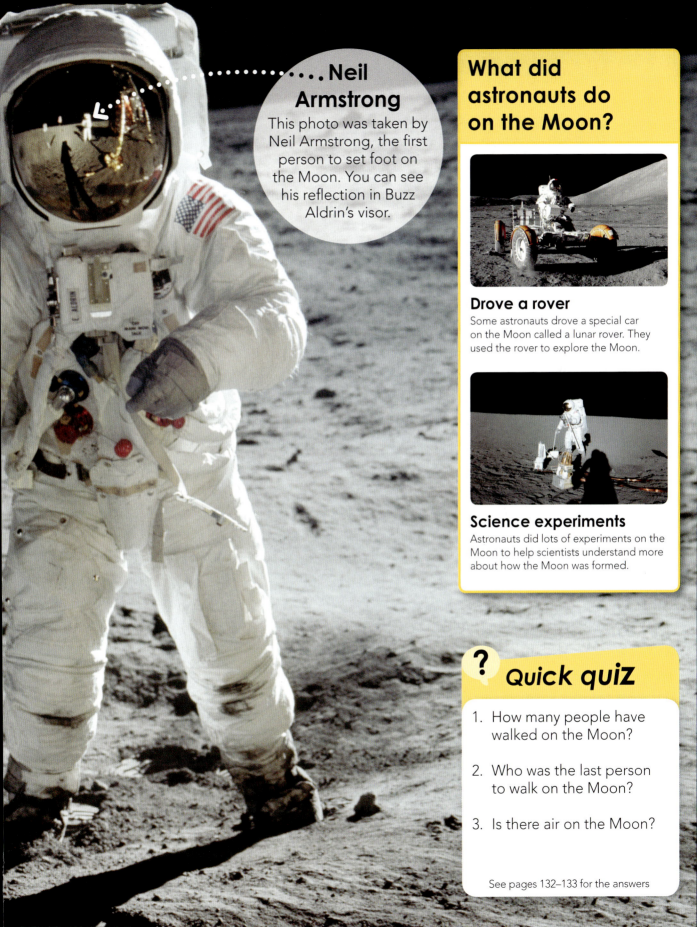

How are rockets launched?

Rockets have engines that burn liquid or solid fuel to make a controlled explosion inside, and this presses on all sides of the engine. However, the engines have holes in the bottom, so here the pressure doubles-back and presses on the top of the engine, sending the rocket up to space, while exhaust (a by-product of the explosion) streams out the bottom.

To get into orbit, a rocket must accelerate from zero to more than 17,400 mph (28,000 kph).

Who were some of the first rocket scientists?

Hermann Oberth
Oberth was a Romanian scientist who is known as one of the "fathers" of modern rocketry. He launched his first rocket in 1931.

Dr. Robert H. Goddard
Goddard was an American who had a talent for inventions. He is known for successfully testing and constructing the first rocket that used liquid fuel.

Fuel and go
Most rockets are made up of two or three stages. When a stage has used up all its fuel, it separates to get rid of the extra weight.

Lightning tower
These towers around the launch pad are designed to stop lightning from hitting and damaging the rocket when it is being prepared for launch.

Hot gas
Lots of exhaust can be seen coming out of the bottom of a rocket as it launches.

? Quick quiz

1. What other name is Hermann Oberth often known by?

2. How many stages do most rockets have?

3. What are the towers around the launch pad used for?

See pages 132–133 for the answers

SPACE EXPLORATION

7. Splashdown
After the spacecraft has reentered the Earth's atmosphere, parachutes open to guide the crew safely to "splashdown" in the ocean.

6. Reentry
When they are nearing Earth, the crew capsule separates from the rest of the craft. A heat shield protects the capsule, so that it doesn't burn up during reentry.

1. Liftoff
The *Saturn V* rocket launches from the Kennedy Space Center, Florida. It is carrying three astronauts and the *Apollo* spacecraft, which comes together in space.

2. To the Moon
In space, the main part of the spacecraft separates from the rocket. Panels open to reveal the Lunar Module, the part that lands on the Moon. The spacecraft turns around and docks with the Lunar Module.

How long does it take to get to the Moon?

During the Apollo Moon landings of 1969–1972, it took astronauts three days to travel to the Moon from the Earth. Each mission followed the same path around the Moon and back again.

? True or false?

1. During the Apollo missions, the whole spacecraft landed on the Moon.

2. It took astronauts on the Apollo missions 10 days to reach the Moon.

3. Parachutes helped the crew of the Apollo missions return safely to Earth.

See pages 132–133 for the answers

Can you see the Earth from the Moon?

Earth rising
This photo of the Earth rising over the Moon was taken by the crew of *Apollo 8*. Some astronauts who visited the Moon described the Earth as looking like a "blue marble" in the sky.

4. Landing on the moon
Once it enters lunar orbit, the Lunar Module, with two of the astronauts onboard, undocks from the main craft and heads for the Moon. Once they have safely touched down, they prepare to walk on the surface.

3. Slowing down
The spacecraft slows down as it nears the Moon. The astronauts make the final preparations for their trip to the surface.

5. Heading home
When they are ready to leave, part of the Lunar Module, with the crew inside, lifts off to rejoin the main craft. The crew fires up their engines to leave lunar orbit.

SPACE EXPLORATION

How do astronauts train for space?

Going into space is not an easy job. It takes years of training. Spacewalking is the most exciting work for astronauts. They train for it by practicing working underwater, which is similar to how it feels to be in space.

Astronaut trainer
This person is an astronaut trainer. They help to guide the astronaut through their underwater tasks.

Space suit
Astronauts train in bulky, protective space suits. This helps the astronauts get used to wearing the suits before they go on real space walks.

Where else do astronauts train?

Vomit Comet
Astronauts can practice floating, just like in space, during flights in a special plane called a reduced-gravity aircraft. It is nicknamed the "Vomit Comet" as it makes some astronauts sick!

Virtual reality
Virtual reality is a digital world that is created by computers. Trainee astronauts wear virtual reality goggles and practice tasks before they go to space.

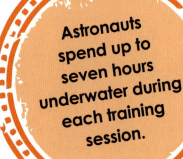

Astronauts spend up to seven hours underwater during each training session.

99

Astronaut
Astronauts need to be fit and healthy, with good eyesight, to go into space. Many are also scientists or engineers.

? True or false?

1. Astronauts only have to train for one week before they go to space.

2. Astronauts can't wear glasses in space.

3. Astronauts practice floating in the "Sick Comet."

See pages 132–133 for the answers

100 SPACE EXPLORATION

? True or false?

1. The first space walk was by Alexey Leonov.
2. Astronauts have visors on their space suits.
3. A life jacket can help stranded astronauts.

See pages 132–133 for the answers

Why do astronauts need space suits?

There is no air to breathe in space and temperatures can quickly change from being very hot to very cold. To stay safe, astronauts must wear a special space suit when they are outside their spacecraft.

Backpack
The backpack contains the astronaut's life-support system. It holds oxygen for the astronaut to breathe and a battery for electrical power.

Inner layers
There are lots of layers to a space suit. Some help to keep the astronaut warm and others help to cool them down.

Helmet and visor
The main part of the helmet is the clear plastic bubble that protects the astronaut's head. There is also a special visor to protect the astronaut's eyes from the Sun's harmful rays.

Drink bag and straw
Sometimes space walks can last for hours, so astronauts get thirsty! They can drink through a straw in their helmet.

Microphone
Spacewalking astronauts have a microphone so they can talk with other astronauts and the support team on Earth.

101

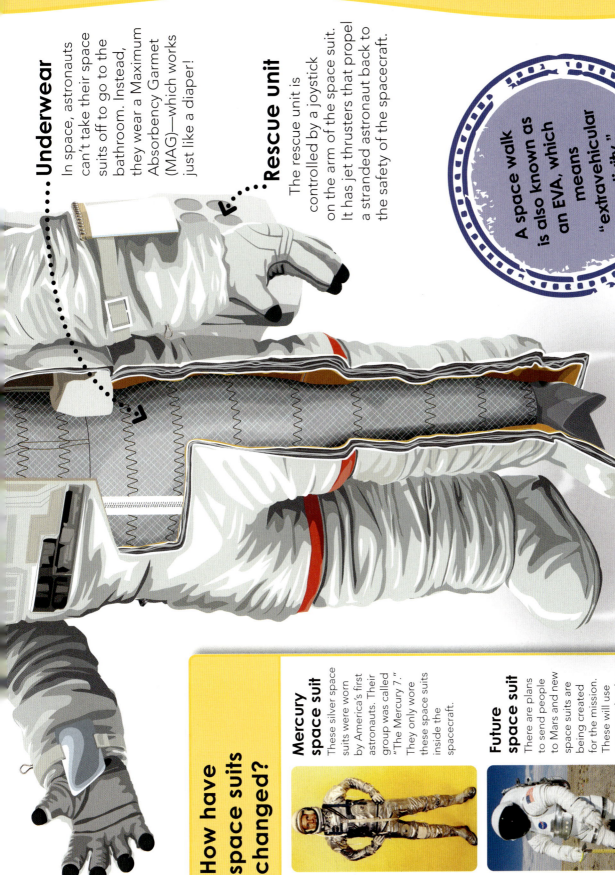

Underwear
In space, astronauts can't take their space suits off to go to the bathroom. Instead, they wear a Maximum Absorbency Garmet (MAG)—which works just like a diaper!

Rescue unit
The rescue unit is controlled by a joystick on the arm of the space suit. It has jet thrusters that propel a stranded astronaut back to the safety of the spacecraft.

A space walk is also known as an EVA, which means "extravehicular activity."

How have space suits changed?

Mercury space suit
These silver space suits were worn by America's first astronauts. Their group was called "The Mercury 7." They only wore these space suits inside the spacecraft.

Future space suit
There are plans to send people to Mars and new space suits are being created for the mission. These will use newer technology than the current space suits.

SPACE EXPLORATION

What was the Space Shuttle?

The Space Shuttle was the first ever reusable spacecraft. It was used by NASA for 30 years to send astronauts into space. Astronauts who flew on it helped to build the International Space Station, repaired the Hubble Space Telescope, and completed lots of important science experiments.

What was it like in the Space Shuttle?

The cockpit
There were five computers with lots of screens (monitors) and control buttons inside the cockpit. These helped the astronauts to fly the shuttle.

Open doors
Astronauts could go outside the main cabin to work in the cargo bay. In the cargo bay, they would have to wear space suits to protect them from the harsh environment of space.

Fuel tank
This contained liquid fuel for the shuttle's main engines.

Living space
This is where the crew would live and work. For launches and landings, the pilot and commander would sit at the front of the Space Shuttle.

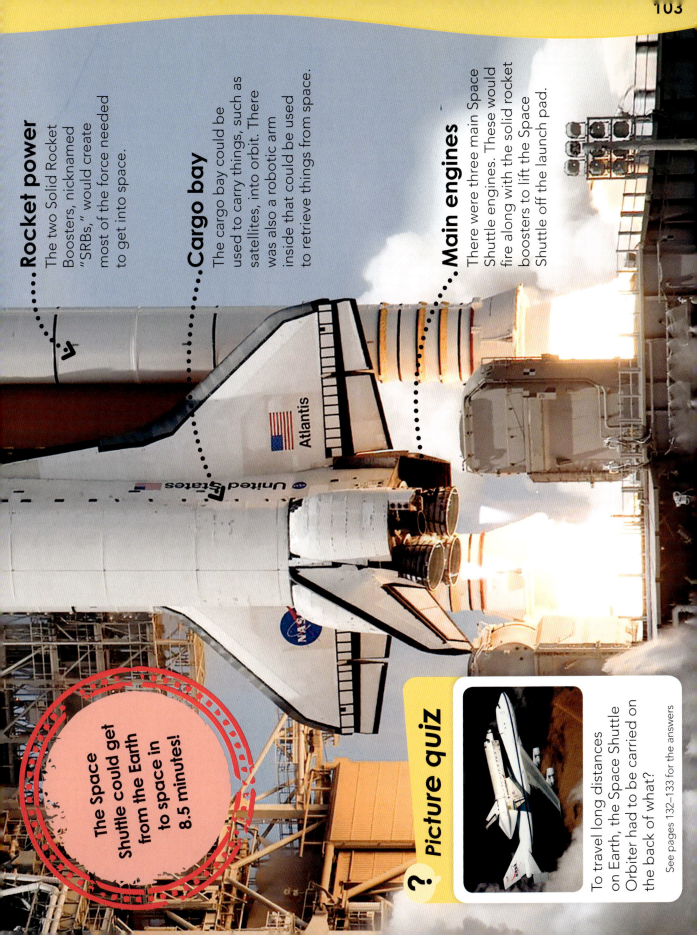

Rocket power
The two Solid Rocket Boosters, nicknamed "SRBs," would create most of the force needed to get into space.

Cargo bay
The cargo bay could be used to carry things, such as satellites, into orbit. There was also a robotic arm inside that could be used to retrieve things from space.

Main engines
There were three main Space Shuttle engines. These would fire along with the solid rocket boosters to lift the Space Shuttle off the launch pad.

The Space Shuttle could get from the Earth to space in 8.5 minutes!

Picture quiz
To travel long distances on Earth, the Space Shuttle Orbiter had to be carried on the back of what?

See pages 132–133 for the answers

104 SPACE EXPLORATION

Ready to depart
The departing astronauts say goodbye and close the hatch to the *Soyuz* spacecraft. They then make sure the *Soyuz* is ready to return them home safely before undocking from the space station.

Journey home
The *Soyuz*'s descent module separates from the spacecraft and it leaves orbit. A special heat shield protects the module as it reenters the Earth's atmosphere. Then, parachutes open 15 minutes before landing.

Landing
One second before landing, engines fire to soften the impact. The crew also sits in specially molded seats, to help make the landing as comfortable as possible.

How do astronauts return to Earth?

Astronauts travel between Earth and the International Space Station in spacecraft like the *Soyuz*. The craft fits three astronauts and takes around three and a half hours to return from the space station back to Earth.

? Quick quiz

1. How long does it take astronauts to get back to the Earth in the *Soyuz*?

2. What do astronauts have to get used to when returning from space?

3. When do the parachutes open on the *Soyuz*?

See pages 132–133 for the answers

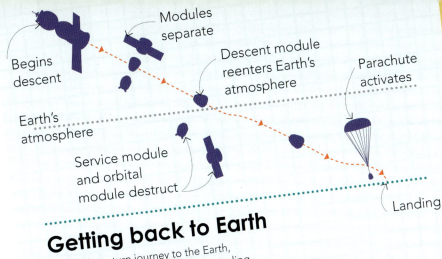

Getting back to Earth

During the return journey to the Earth, the *Soyuz* has to slow down from traveling at 16,750 mph (27,000 kph) to zero!

Back on Earth
The astronauts are now out of the spacecraft and back on Earth. After being in space for so long, it takes them a little while to adjust to the gravity on the Earth.

Exit team
A team tracks where the descent module lands and rushes to find the astronauts to help them out of the spacecraft.

How did the Space Shuttle land?

Runway finish
When the Space Shuttle flew, it would return to the Earth like a glider and land on a runway. A special drag chute would help slow it down as it landed.

Where do astronauts live in space?

Today, the International Space Station (ISS) is where astronauts live, sleep, exercise, and work in space. It is the biggest object ever flown in space and is the first step toward exploring deeper into our solar system.

Kibo module
The Japanese *Kibo* module is one of the places where experiments are carried out. The module has a small chamber, which astronauts can use to put experiments outside the ISS.

Solar panels
The best source of energy in space is the Sun. Solar panels are used to collect sunlight that is then changed into electricity.

Soyuz
The *Soyuz* capsule carries astronauts to and from the ISS. Astronauts returning to Earth travel in spacecraft like the *Soyuz*.

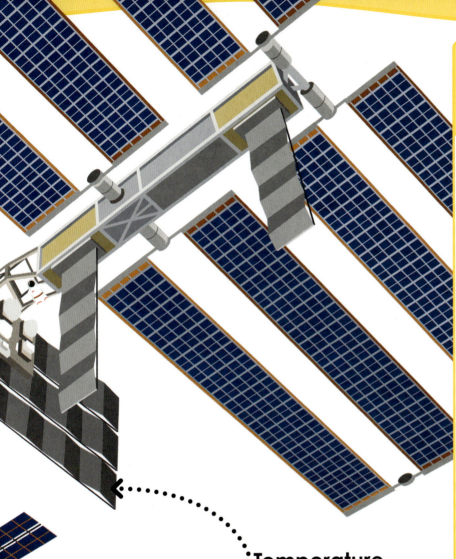

Temperature control

The ISS is equipped with a temperature control system to keep the station's temperature comfortable for the astronauts inside. Without it, the station's Sun-facing side could reach temperatures of 248°F (120°C), and its dark side could be as cold as -238°F (-150°C).

Zvezda module

The *Zvezda* module is a Russian module on the ISS. It provides life-support systems, as well as living quarters for two astronauts.

What do astronauts do in space?

Space walks
Sometimes astronauts go for space walks to repair and maintain the outside of the International Space Station.

Science experiments
Astronauts study how materials and living things behave in space. What they learn can help how we live on the Earth.

? Quick quiz

1. How hot would the ISS get without controlling its temperature?

2. What do the solar panels on the space station do?

3. What is the *Kibo* module used for?

See pages 132–133 for the answers

Why do astronauts float in space?

In space, astronauts don't walk around on the floor like people do on the Earth. Instead, they float! This is because they do not feel the effect of gravity, which is the force that pulls you toward the ground on the Earth. This state is called microgravity, and it makes things seem to be weightless.

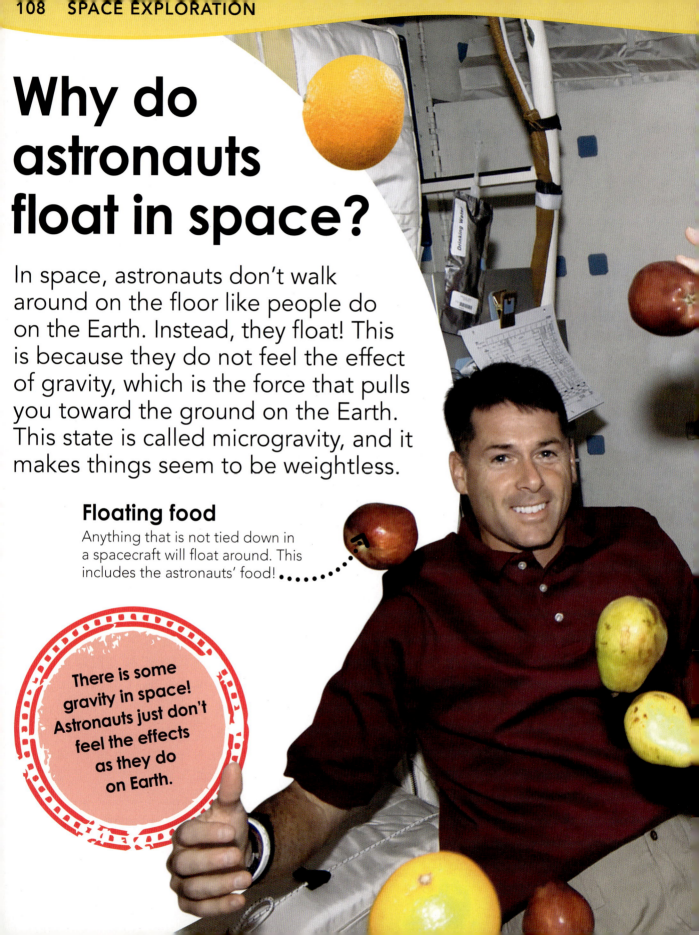

Floating food
Anything that is not tied down in a spacecraft will float around. This includes the astronauts' food!

There is some gravity in space! Astronauts just don't feel the effects as they do on Earth.

? Quick quiz

1. What is microgravity?
2. Can humans float on the Earth?
3. Would you float on the Moon?

See pages 132–133 for the answers

Super strength

Weightlessness in space lets astronauts look as though they are super strong. They can lift objects, such as big pieces of equipment, that would be far too heavy for them to move on the Earth.

How do astronauts stay fit and healthy in space?

Exercise
With very little gravity to push against, a person's bones and muscles soon become weak. Astronauts exercise every day to stay healthy and help avoid any problems when they return to the Earth and its gravity.

Sleeping quarters
In space, there is no up and down. Astronauts can attach their sleeping bags wherever they want—even on the ceiling! They have to strap themselves in too or they will float away.

What do astronauts eat in space?

Astronauts living in space need to eat three meals a day. The food they eat is similar to ours, but it needs to be "cooked" and eaten differently. Astronauts aren't allowed crumbly food such as bread because the crumbs can float around and clog up the spacecraft's air vents!

Making dinner

Many space meals are dried. To prepare them, astronauts inject hot water into the packages and wait several minutes before eating them.

Beef patty — Add hot water and wait 10–15 minutes.

Trail mix

Cheddar cheese spread

Beefsteak

Cashews

Astronauts use liquid salt and pepper so the grains don't float around and get in their eyes.

What other things are difficult to do in space?

Brushing teeth
There's no running water in space, so astronauts soak their toothbrushes before cleaning their teeth. After brushing, they swallow their toothpaste because there's nowhere to spit it out.

Using the bathroom
Going to the bathroom is very different in space. Astronauts need to strap their legs down, so they don't float away. A space toilet works a bit like a vacuum cleaner, sucking human waste away!

Eating food
Astronauts don't use plates, knives, and forks. Instead, they can use spoons, "sip" their food through plastic tubes, or eat it as it floats in front of them.

Creamed spinach
Add hot water and wait 5–10 minutes.

Crackers

Vacuum-sealed
Many space meals are vacuum-sealed. This means that all the air is sucked out of the packet, so the food stays fresh for a long time.

Knead before opening.

Candy-coated peanuts

Orangeade

? Quick quiz

1. How many meals do astronauts need a day?

2. How do astronauts eat their food?

3. How is most food packaged for astronauts to eat in space?

See pages 132–133 for the answers

What is mission control?

The work that astronauts do would be impossible without mission control. It is a place where many people work to help space missions and astronauts in space. People work in mission control every hour of the day, every day of the year.

What jobs do people have in mission control?

Spacecraft communicator
The person at mission control who communicates with astronauts in space is called a CAPCOM, or capsule communicator.

Flight surgeon
A flight surgeon is a doctor who gives astronauts advice on how to stay healthy. If an astronaut gets hurt in space, the surgeon will tell them what they need to do to recover.

Keeping watch
There are lots of big screens, or monitors, in mission control. They let the people working there keep a close watch on the spacecraft and the astronauts.

Support teams
Teams of people on the ground provide support for astronauts working in space. They help astronauts with many jobs, including space walks and experiments.

Instant information
The ground team at mission control gather data from the spacecraft. They study it to help make decisions about what to do next on the mission.

Quick quiz

1. What does CAPCOM stand for?

2. What does a flight surgeon do?

3. How many hours a day is mission control open?

See pages 132–133 for the answers

What happens when things go wrong in space?

Sometimes things don't go as planned when astronauts are in space. However, lots of people back on Earth work with astronauts to help them get through any emergencies, as happened with the Apollo 13 mission…

Apollo 13's journey

After finding the problems with their spacecraft, the crew of *Apollo 13* had to act fast. To get back home, they had to use the Moon's gravity to slingshot them safely back to Earth.

1. Apollo 13 was launched on April 11, 1970.

2. About 200,000 miles (320,000 km) from Earth, a fire started on the spacecraft and the mission was aborted.

3. Apollo 13 went around the far side of the Moon once before heading home.

4. Close to Earth, the crew had to power up the spacecraft.

5. Splashdown! Apollo 13 arrived home safely on April 17, 1970.

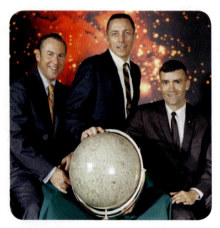

Crew
Apollo 13 was meant to be the third crewed spacecraft to land on the moon. The American astronauts on this trip were Jim Lovell, Jack Swigert, and Fred Haise.

What happened?
On the way to the Moon, a spark in an oxygen tank caused an explosion on the spacecraft. It wouldn't be safe to land on the Moon, so the astronauts had to return home quickly.

Solving problems
There were lots of problems to solve to get the astronauts home safely. Mission control worked hard until they figured out the best ways to keep the crew safe.

How do astronauts stay safe in space?

Soyuz spacecraft
The *Soyuz* spaceship is a Russian craft that takes astronauts to and from the International Space Station (ISS). If they need to leave the ISS in an emergency, astronauts can use it to return to Earth. This spacecraft is known as a Crew Return Vehicle (CRV).

Launch Escape System
Rockets have a Launch Escape System (LES). If anything goes wrong soon after the rocket's launch from Earth, the LES engines fire and carry the crew capsule a safe distance away from the rocket.

Arriving home
Three days after the mission was aborted, or cut short, the crew splashed down safely in the Pacific Ocean. They were given a hero's welcome.

? True or false?

1. There were four astronauts on *Apollo 13*.

2. *Apollo 13* landed on the Moon.

3. A Launch Escape System can help keep a crew safe.

See pages 132–133 for the answers

SPACE EXPLORATION

Have we been to Mars?

Humans haven't yet been to Mars because we don't have the technology to do so. However, we have sent robots to investigate the Red Planet. *Curiosity* is a NASA rover that has been exploring Mars since August 2012. It is helping us understand if life could have existed there.

Cameras
Curiosity has 17 cameras. They take pictures of Mars and some of them act as the rover's "eyes."

Wheels
Wide wheels help the rover grip to the bumpy martian surface. They do not have tires because they could get punctured too easily.

What's next for Mars?

More robots
The *ExoMars* rover is a European rover that will travel to Mars in the near future. It will drill into the surface of Mars to see if life could exist underground.

Human missions
There are plans to send people to Mars. Humans will be able to discover more than current robotic missions, because they can do a lot more than robots.

Curiosity only travels 1.5 in (3.8 cm) each second.

? Picture quiz

This image was taken at sunset on Mars. Can you guess what the white circle is?

See pages 132–133 for the answers

Robotic arm
This arm holds tools to collect and examine rocks for scientists back on Earth. It has joints just like a human arm.

Why do we put satellites in space?

Traveling around the Earth high above you are hundreds and hundreds of satellites. These are machines that have been launched into space to orbit the Earth. Satellites do many useful jobs such as helping us forecast the weather, letting us use cell phones, and taking pictures from space.

What else do satellites do?

Study space
Some satellites work as telescopes. The Kepler space telescope scans space to look for Earthlike planets.

Look at the Earth
A lot of satellites look back at the Earth. This satellite is called CALIPSO and it monitors the clouds and weather on Earth.

Antenna
The antenna sends out signals to the Earth. It can also receive signals from the Earth.

Solar panel
This flat, rectangular "wing" is a solar panel. It uses sunlight to make electricity, which powers the satellite's equipment.

Satellites travel very fast. Some can orbit the Earth 14 times in one day!

Picture quiz

In October 1957, the first satellite was put into orbit. What was its name?

See pages 132–133 for the answers

Antenna dish
A lot of satellites in space are used for communications. Their antenna dishes receive and pass on telephone, television, and Internet signals, like other antennas do.

How far have we traveled in space?

Humans have sent spacecraft to visit every planet in the solar system, as well as the dwarf planet, Pluto. We have also visited the asteroid belt, landed on a comet, and seen the moons of other planets up close.

Jupiter
Several spacecraft have visited the gas giant Jupiter. They have studied its Great Red Spot, or storm, photographed its many moons, and helped us understand more about this huge planet.

Can spacecraft get lost?

Yes, and sometimes found again! Contact with the lander *Philae* was lost after it landed on a comet. However, scientists later found it hidden in the shadow of a cliff on the comet.

Beyond the solar system
The *Voyager 1* spacecraft has traveled so far through space that it has now entered interstaller space. It is still sending information back to scientists.

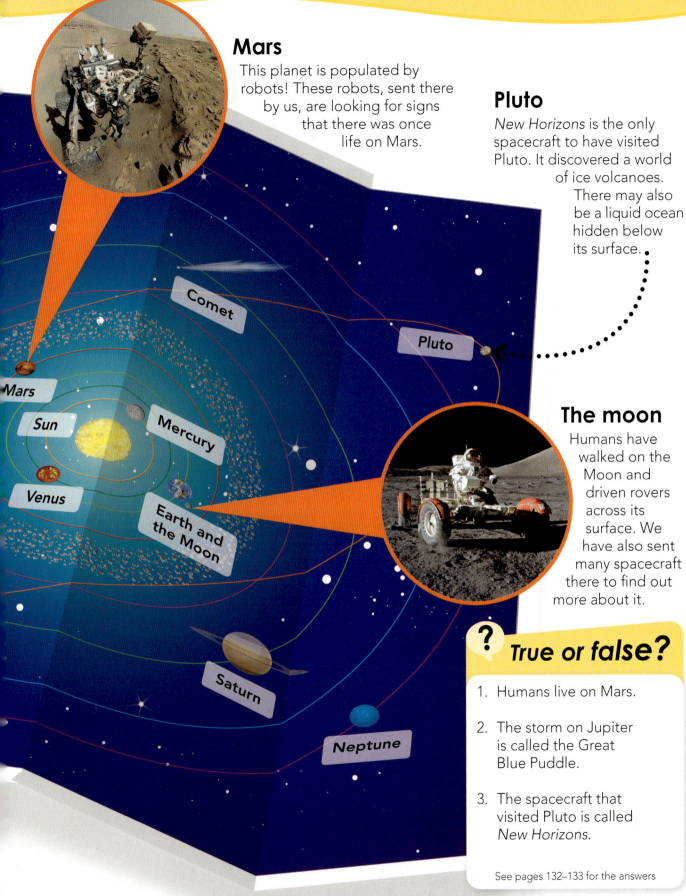

What is space junk?

Everywhere humans go, they leave garbage—and that includes space! Space junk is the garbage left over from things we have sent into space. These things are either broken or no longer needed. There are millions of pieces of space junk orbiting our planet.

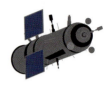

Parts of rockets
Space junk includes parts of rockets that were used to launch satellites into space. These parts are left orbiting Earth.

? Picture quiz

How often do you think a piece of space junk falls to Earth?

See pages 132–133 for the answers

How can we clean up space?

Locate the junk
Big telescopes on the ground are able to locate space junk orbiting Earth. They are powerful enough to detect pieces of junk as small as 0.4 in (1 cm) across.

Collect the junk
These grids are junk collectors that are being tested outside the ISS. The grids are made up of trays of a spongelike gel, which traps tiny pieces of space junk orbiting Earth.

Astronauts' equipment
Sometimes when astronauts go on space walks, they "drop" things, such as cameras. These things float away as space junk.

Old satellites
There are lots of old satellites in space. Sometimes they crash into each other, creating even more junk!

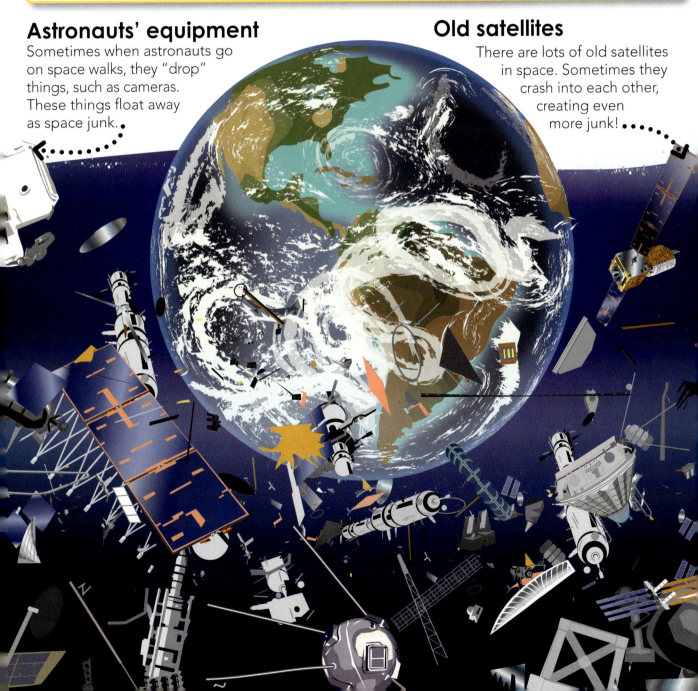

Is there anyone else out there?

So far we have only found life on Earth, but the universe could be full of life we haven't yet discovered. An organization called SETI (Search for Extra-Terrestrial Intelligence) is trying to find out if there is anyone else out there.

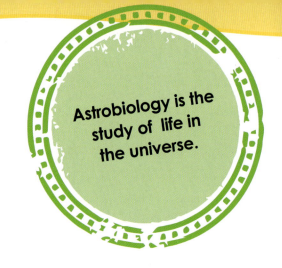

Astrobiology is the study of life in the universe.

Scanning the sky
Scientists use a group of radio telescopes to scan the sky for signals that might be coming from space.

Allen Telescope Array
This collection of radio telescopes is called an "array." It is used by SETI to hunt for signals, which may come from life elsewhere in the universe.

What messages have we sent out to space?

Arecibo message
Beamed to a group of thousands of stars, this message was the most powerful broadcast ever deliberately sent into space. It contains details of life on Earth and a stick figure drawing of a human being.

Golden record
The *Voyager 1* and *2* spacecraft have onboard records that explain where they came from. These include images and sounds from life on Earth.

? Picture quiz

The frozen moon, Europa, could support life. Which planet does it orbit?

See pages 132–133 for the answers

Telescope antennas
These big antennas collect the radio signals, which is one type of light coming from space.

What is space mining?

Space is full of things that could be useful to humans. Asteroids, for example, have the ingredients that we could use to make rocket fuel. In the future, humans may mine, or dig, on asteroids to find these ingredients and help us explore farther into space.

An asteroid the size of a house could contain metals that are worth millions of dollars.

Asteroid riches
There are lots of precious metals in asteroids, which could be mined and returned to Earth. There is also oxygen, which could be used to make fuel for spacecraft.

Mining spacecraft
Special spacecraft can survey asteroids to find out which ones contain materials that could be mined.

Where else can we mine in space?

The Moon
The Moon has the potential to be mined. Future spacecraft could even refuel at the Moon on the way to other planets.

Distant worlds
As we explore deeper into the solar system, spacecraft will be able to mine faraway worlds for useful materials.

? True or false?

1. One day, we could mine asteroids.

2. Mined oxygen could be useful to future astronauts.

3. Some metals can be found on asteroids.

See pages 132–133 for the answers

128 SPACE EXPLORATION

Can you go on vacation to space?

So far, fewer than 600 people have traveled into space. Of those, only a few have not been scientists. At the moment, lots of companies are developing new ways to send us on space vacations.

Wish you were there...
One day you could be able to see the Earth from space, and in the future, people could even explore faraway worlds in the solar system.

The first space tourist was American Dennis Tito. In 2001, he paid $20 million for a trip to the ISS!

Greetings from Europa

PASSPORT

Planet Earth

A view of Earth

How else will we get to space?

Vacationers
Virgin Galactic is one of a few companies developing spaceships to send tourists into space. The trips would last a few hours and passengers would get to feel weightless.

Space cruise
Using pressurized capsules, high-altitude balloon rides may take tourists to the edge of space. This is *Voyager*, made by World View Enterprises.

? Quick quiz

1. Who was the first space tourist?

2. How much did the first space tourist pay to go to space?

3. In the future, how might tourists travel to the edge of space?

See pages 132–133 for the answers

SPACE EXPLORATION

Moon base
A future Moon base could use some of the Moon's rocks for the buildings where astronauts would live and work.

Will we go back to the Moon?

People haven't visited the Moon since 1972. However, since then we have sent spacecraft there and learned a lot more about the Moon. There are plans for astronauts to return to the Moon in the future and build a base, where they could live and work.

The Moon is moving away from the Earth at a rate of about 1½ in (4 cm) a year.

Quick quiz

1. When did people last visit the Moon?
2. How will people breathe on the Moon?
3. Where in space are inflatable bases being tested?

See pages 132–133 for the answers

Space suit
People living in the Moon base will still need a space suit with an air supply to go outside. This is because there is no air to breathe on the Moon.

What's in the future for space exploration?

New rockets
New rockets will allow humans to explore farther into space than ever before. The SpaceX *Falcon Heavy* is a new rocket that will be one of the most powerful in the world when it launches.

Inflatable bases
Future bases in space could be made from special materials that can be inflated, or blown up like a balloon in space. A base like this is being tested on the International Space Station.

Answers

Page 9 1) An area where baby stars form. 2) People have been going into space since 1961. 3) Yes, the Earth and everything else in the universe is in space.

Page 10 1) a. The Karman Line is 62 miles (100 km) above the Earth's surface. 2) c.

Page 13 1) False. The universe is around 13.8 billion years old. 2) True. 3) False. The universe is still growing.

Page 15 1) The Milky Way. 2) Roughly, more than one million Earths can fit inside the Sun. 3) The Moon is Earth's closest neighbor in space.

Page 17 1) Triton. Temperatures on this moon can drop to -391°F (-235°C) 2) The Boomerang Nebula.

Page 19 1) True. 2) True. 3) False. It takes the Moon 27 days 7 hours and 43 minutes to orbit the Earth.

Page 21 1) Spacewalking astronauts wear microphones so that they can talk to each other. 2) A vacuum is an area with almost nothing in it. 3) No, there is no air in space.

Page 25 1) a. 2) b.

Page 26 1) False. There are four rocky planets. 2) True. 3) True.

Page 28 The blue whale.

Page 30 The Earth.

Page 33 1) True. 2) False. Mars has a north and a south pole. 3) True.

Page 35 1) False. Jupiter, Uranus, and Neptune also have rings. 2) True. Saturn has many rings. 3) True.

Page 37 1) Pluto is a dwarf planet. 2) Five dwarf planets have been discovered. They are Ceres, Eris, Haumea, Makemake, and Pluto. 3) Pluto has five moons. They are Charon, Hydra, Kerberos, Nix, and Styx.

Page 39 1) The hottest part of the Sun is its center, or core. 2) Solar flares are gigantic eruptions of energy from the surface of the Sun. 3) The Earth is about 93 million miles (150 million km) away from the Sun.

Page 41 1) False. The Moon orbits the Earth. 2) True. 3) True.

Page 43 1) Usually just a few minutes, but sometimes as long as seven minutes. 2) Because the Sun is so bright that it can blind anyone who looks at it without glasses. 3) A partial eclipse.

Page 45 Mars.

Page 47 1) Meteoroids are found in space. 2) Arizona. 3) A meteorite is a piece of space rock that has fallen to Earth.

Page 49 1) True. 2) False. It is the comet Tempel-Tuttle. 3) False. It is not a star, but a piece of space dust or rock that is falling to Earth.

Page 51 1) False. Comets only develop tails when they pass near the Sun. 2) True. It is usually called the nucleus, but it is sometimes described as a "dirty snowball." 3) False. The lander was called *Philae*. The spacecraft, *Rosetta*, ended its mission in 2016 by crashing into a comet after sending its last pictures and data back to Earth.

Page 53 Yes, the asteroid Ida (shown in the picture) has a tiny moon called Dactyl orbiting it (the dot in the picture).

Page 55 1) True. 2) False. 3) True

Page 57 1) True. The best time of year to see them is during winter. 2) True. They can be green, purple, pink, red, or yellow. 3) True.

Page 59 1) False. Mercury is the closest planet to the Sun. 2) True. 3) False. Venus is covered in gray rocks.

Page 63 It's a spiral galaxy.

Page 65 1) True. These clouds are called nebulas. 2) False. The Sun is about 4.6 billion years old.

Page 67 1) True. There are red and blue giants. 2) True. There are red, white, black, and brown dwarfs. 3) False. Our Sun is an average star.

Page 69 1) The speed of light is 186,500 miles (300,000 km) per second. 2) Light from the sun takes more than eight minutes to reach the Earth. 3) It takes the International Space Station around 90 minutes to orbit the Earth.

Page 71 1) A black hole doesn't look like anything—it's invisible. 2) Gravity is the force that pulls things into a black hole. 3) Time goes slower near a black hole.

Page 73 1) c. 2) c.

Page 75 1) a. The arms of some galaxies are made of stars. 2) c. A galaxy that has no particular shape is called an irregular galaxy.

Page 77 1) Yes, you can see planets in the night sky. Mercury, Venus, Mars, Jupiter, and Saturn are the brightest planets that can be seen from Earth without a telescope. The planets can be seen at different times of the year. 2) Patterns of stars are called constellations. 3) The brightest object that you can see in the night sky is the Moon.

Page 79 1) Yes, other stars often have planets. 2) Rogue planets are planets that don't orbit a star. 3) Planets that orbit other stars are called exoplanets.

Page 81 1) True. 2) False. Quasars are the brightest things in the universe. 3) True.

Page 85 1) A telescope is something that we can use to see farther into space. 2) Galileo made his telescope in 1609. 3) The Yepun telescope is more than 26 ft (8 m) wide.

Page 87 When John Glenn went into space for the second time, he was 77 years old, which made him the oldest person to have been in space.

Page 89 1) The first dog in space was called Laika. 2) The first animals in space were fruit flies. 3) Ham the chimpanzee was four years old when he went into space.

Page 91 The first person to set foot on the Moon was Neil Armstrong.

Page 93 1) Twelve people have walked on the Moon. 2) Eugene Ceman—he was actually the 11th person to step on the Moon, but the last person to leave it. 3) No, scientists have found a thin layer of gas on the Moon, but no air.

Page 95 1) Hermann Oberth is often called one of the fathers of modern rocketry. 2) Most rockets are made up of two or three stages. 3) The towers around the launch pad are to protect the rocket from lightning strikes.

Page 96 1) False. Only the Lunar Module landed on the Moon. 2) False. It took astronauts on the Apollo missions three days to reach the Moon. 3) True. A parachute helped to guide the crew to safety.

Page 99 1) False. Training for space takes years. 2) False. Lots of astronauts wear glasses. As long as their vision is perfect when they wear them, they are still able to go to space. 3) False. They practice in the "Vomit Comet."

Page 100 1) True. In 1965 Alexey Leonov was the first person to go on a space walk. 2) True. The visors protect their eyes from the Sun's harmful rays. 3) False. A rescue unit will help stranded astronauts.

Page 103 To travel on Earth the Space Shuttle Orbiter had to be carried on the back of an airplane.

Page 104 1) It takes astronauts three and a half hours to return to Earth in the *Soyuz*. 2) Astronauts have to get used to gravity when they return from space. 3) The parachutes on *Soyuz* open 15 minutes before landing.

Page 107 1) If the temperature was not controlled, the ISS could get as hot as 248°F (120°C). 2) The solar panels create electricity. 3) The Kibo module is used to conduct experiments on the ISS.

Page 109 1) Microgravity is the state in space where people and things seem to be weightless and can float. 2) Humans cannot float in the air on Earth because gravity pulls us to the ground. We can, however, float in water! 3) No, the Moon has its own gravity, but it's much weaker than the Earth's gravity. You would weigh less on the Moon, and if you jumped, you would be able to jump higher than on the Earth. You wouldn't float away, however, but land back on the ground more slowly than on the Earth.

Page 111 1) Astronauts need to eat three meals a day. 2) Astronauts can use a spoon, "sip" their food through a tube, or eat it as it floats in front of them. 3) Most food that astronauts eat in space is vacuum-sealed.

Page 113 1) CAPCOM stands for capsule communicator. 2) A flight surgeon is a doctor who gives astronauts advice on how to stay healthy. 3) Mission control is open 24 hours a day, 7 days of the week, every day of the year.

Page 115 1) False. There were three astronauts on *Apollo 13*. 2) False. There was a problem and *Apollo 13* had to return to Earth before landing on the Moon. 3) True. A Launch Escape System can help carry the crew away from a rocket.

Page 117 The white circle is the Sun.

Page 119 The first satellite was called *Sputnik 1*.

Page 121 1) False. Only robots, that were sent by humans, can be found on Mars. 2) False. The storm on Jupiter is called the Great Red Spot. 3) True. The spacecraft, *New Horizons*, visited Pluto in 2015.

Page 122 At least one tiny piece of space junk falls to Earth every day.

Page 125 Europa orbits Jupiter.

Page 127 1) True. 2) True. Oxygen mined from asteroids could be used to make rocket fuel and many other things. 3) True. Many different metals can be found on asteroids.

Page 129 1) Dennis Tito was the first space tourist. 2) Dennis Tito paid $20 million to visit the International Space Station. 3) In the future, tourists might be able to travel to the edge of space in a balloon, such as *Voyager*, or in a spaceship.

Page 131 1) People last visited the Moon in 1972. 2) People will have a supply of air so that they can breathe on the Moon. 3) Inflatable bases are being tested on the International Space Station. One such base is called the Bigelow Expandable Activity Module (BEAM) and can expand by five times its compressed size in just 45 minutes.

Quiz your friends!

Who knows the most about space? Test your friends and family with these tricky questions. See pages 136–137 for the answers.

Questions

1. Which planet has the most moons?

4. How long does it take for the **Earth** to complete one full **orbit** around the **sun**?

7. **How old is our Sun?**

10. What crashes into the **Moon** and creates **huge craters** on its surface?

2. Do **Mercury** and **Venus** have any moons?

3. How fast does the **Earth** rotate?

5. Which was the first **rover** to land on Mars?

6. What is the **largest telescope** ever launched?

8. Which planet has the biggest ocean?

9. Which metals can be found in **meteorites**?

11. What is the **average temperature** on **Neptune**?

12. What is the **largest object** in the asteroid belt?

13. How many people live on the **International Space Station (ISS)** at a time?

14. Can you see twinkling stars from **the surface of the Moon**?

15. Which **spacecraft** was the first to land on a **comet**?

Answers

1. Saturn

4. The Earth takes **365 days** to complete one full orbit around the Sun.

2. **Mercury** and **Venus** do not have any moons!

3. The Earth rotates on its axis at a speed of up to **1,037 mph (1,670 kph)**.

5. In 1997, the ***Sojourner*** rover became the first rover to **land** on the surface of Mars.

6. **The Hubble Space Telescope**

7. The Sun is **4.6 billion years** old.

8. Earth

9. **Nickel** and **iron** are metals that can be found in meteorites.

10. Meteorites

11. **Neptune** averages a temperature of around -346°F (-210°C), making it the **coldest planet in the solar system**.

12. Ceres

13. **Six astronauts** can live and work on the ISS at the same time.

14. No, because the Moon has **no atmosphere**.

15. The ***Philae*** **lander**.

Glossary

accelerate
When something, often a vehicle, quickly picks up speed

altitude
How high above sea level or the ground something is

array
Display or range of a certain thing

asteroid
Small, rocky object that orbits the Sun

atmosphere
Layers of gas that surround a planet

atoms
Building blocks of elements. Everything is made from atoms

aurora
Light displays caused by particles from the Sun that interact with the atmosphere of planets, typically at the north and south poles.

big bang
Theory of how the universe has evolved, starting very hot and dense and expanding and cooling over time.

black hole
Massive object in space with a strong force of gravity that nothing can escape from, not even light

comet
Object made of dust and ice that orbits around the Sun, developing a tail as it gets closer to the Sun

constellation
Group of stars that forms a pattern

corona
Outer atmosphere of the Sun

cosmonaut
Human space traveler, mainly used to refer to Russian astronauts

crater
Bowl-shaped dent on the surface of a planet or other object in space, caused by the collision with a space rock

crew
Group of people who work on a spacecraft

dense
When something is thick and tightly packed, such as a dense fog

dwarf planet
Object in space that is similar to a planet but is smaller and has not cleared its orbit

eclipse
When an object is in the shadow of another object or another object passes between it and the viewer and it is obscured from view

exoplanet
Planet that orbits a star other than the Sun

galaxy
Huge group of stars, gas, and dust held together by gravity

glacier
Large mass of ice found on land

gravity
Force that pulls things toward each other

habitable zone
Area around a star that has conditions that are suitable for life

ice cap
Area of ice that usually covers the north and south poles of a planet

Kármán Line
Imaginary line that is 62 miles (100 km) above the surface of the Earth and marks where space begins

Kuiper Belt
Region of ice and rock that lies beyond Neptune

light-year
Distance that light can travel in one Earth year

lunar
Word used to relate to the Moon

matter
Stuff that all things are made of

meteor
When a meteoroid burns up as it enters the Earth's atmosphere, appearing as a streak of light in the sky

meteorite
Meteoroid that lands on a planet or Moon's surface

meteoroid
Particle of rock, metal, or ice traveling through space

meteor shower
Result of lots of meteors in the sky

microgravity
When things appear weightless in space

molecular cloud
Dense cloud in space where stars can form

moon
Object made of rock or rock and ice that orbits a planet or asteroid

nebula
Cloud of gas and dust in space where stars are born

north pole
The most northern point of a planet

nucleus
Central and most important part of something such as a comet or black hole

orbit
Path an object takes around another when pulled by its gravity

ozone layer
Area in the Earth's atmosphere that protects the surface from the Sun's harmful rays

parent star
Star that provides heat and light for the planets orbiting around it

particles
Extremely small parts of a solid, liquid, or gas

pioneer
Person who is one of the first to explore a new place

planet
Large, spherical object that orbits a star

pressurized
Something that is sealed with air that humans are able to breathe

rogue planet
Planet that does not orbit a star

rover
Vehicle that is driven on the surface of a planet or Moon

satellite
Object that orbits another larger object. It can be natural or made by people

solar flare
Gigantic eruptions of energy from the surface of the Sun

space probe
Uncrewed spacecraft designed to study objects in space and send information back to Earth

space suit
Sealed, protective clothing worn by an astronaut to protect them in space

space station
Large spacecraft that is usually occupied by humans, where experiments can be conducted

space walk
When an astronaut in space is outside a spacecraft, usually to repair or test equipment

star
Huge, glowing sphere of gas that creates energy in its core

sunspots
Dark spots that appear on the Sun's surface

supernova
Explosion that happens in space when a star dies

telescope
Instrument used to look at distant objects

test pilot
Pilot who flies aircraft to test how they work

tourist
Person who visits a place for a vacation

toxic
Poisonous

universe
All space and everything in it

vacuum
Area with nothing in it, not even air

virtual reality
Environment that has been created by computers. It appears to be real and can be seen, but nothing in it is solid, or physical

visor
Part of a helmet that can be moved up and down over a person's face

wormhole
Possible passage in space that can connect two places that are far apart. Scientists have not yet found a wormhole, but do think they could exist

Index

A
accretion disk 81
Aldrin, Buzz 87, 91, 92–3
Allen Telescope Array 124
Anders, Bill 86–7
animals
 on Earth 28, 29
 in space 88–9
antennas 118–19
Apollo missions 87, 92–3, 96–7
Apollo 13 114
Armstrong, Neil 87, 91, 92–3
asteroid belt 52–3, 120
asteroids 24, 44, 52, 53, 126
astrobiology 124
astronauts 8, 86–7, 90–93
 activities in space 107
 eating in space 110–11
 health and fitness 109
 living in space 102, 106–7
 mission control 112–13
 on Moon 87, 91, 92–3
 problems in space 114–15
 return to Earth 104–5
 return to Moon 130–31
 space junk 123
 space suits 98, 100–101
 training 98–9
 weightlessness 11, 98, 108–9
atmosphere
 Earth 11, 76
 ice and gas giants 27
 Mars 32
 Venus 58, 59
atoms 12, 13
auroras 31, 56–7
average stars 72

B
backpacks 100
balloons, high-altitude 129
Barringer Crater 46–7
bases, inflatable 131
Bean, Alan 92
big bang 12, 13
black dwarfs 73
black holes 70–71, 73, 75
 supermassive 80–81
blue giants 67
blue supergiants 67
Boomerang Nebula 17
Borman, Frank 86–7

C
CALIPSO 118
CAPCOM 112
Carina Nebula 65
Cassini Division 35
Cassini–Huygens spacecraft 54
Ceres 53
Cernan, Eugene 92
CFBDSIR 2149-0403 78
chimpanzees 88
clouds (Venus) 59
Collins, Michael 87
comas 50
comets 24, 49
 landing on 120
 tails 50–51
Conrad, Pete 92
constellations 77
core 26, 27
craters 46–7
Crew Return Vehicle (CRV) 115
crust 26

D
dark spots (Neptune) 31
deep space 60–81
dogs 88, 89
drinking 100
Duke, Charles 92
dust storms 32
dwarf planets 24, 25, 36, 37, 53

E
Eagle Nebula 64–5
Earth 15, 25, 26
 auroras 56
 from space 54–5, 97
 life on 28–9
 meteors 46–7
 orbit of Sun 18
 satellite monitoring 118
 temperature 17

eating 110–11
elliptical galaxies 74
emergencies, space 114–15
Enceladus 45
energy 28, 29
Europa 44, 125
exercise 109
exoplanets 27, 78–9
exosphere 10

F
Falcon Heavy 131
flight surgeons 112
food 110–11
fruit flies 88
fuel, rocket 94, 95, 102, 126

G
Gagarin, Yuri 86, 91
galaxies
   formation of 13
   number of 63, 74
   shape of 74
Galilei, Galileo 85
Ganymede 44
gas giants 25, 26, 27
Glenn, John 87

Goddard, Robert H. 94
Golden record 125
gravity 11
   black holes 70
Great Red Spot (Jupiter) 30, 120
Great White Spot (Saturn) 31

H
habitable zone 28, 79
Haise, Fred 114
Haumea 37
HD 189733b 27
heat shields 104
helmets 100
Horsehead Nebula 65
Hubble Space Telescope 10, 18, 63, 102

I
ice giants 26, 27
International Space Station (ISS) 10, 11, 54, 69, 102, 104, 106–7
internet signals 119
Io 45

irregular galaxies 74
Irwin, James 92

J
Juno spacecraft 69
Jupiter 15, 25, 26, 27
   auroras 56
   exploration 120
   moons 44–5
   rings 35
   stripes 30–31

K
Karman Line 11
Kennedy, John F. 91
Kepler 62f 79
Kepler 186f 27
Kepler space telescope 118
Kepler's Supernova 73
Kibo module 106
Kuiper Belt 25, 36, 37

L
Laika 89, 90
laser beams 84
Launch Escape System 115

Leonid meteor shower 49
Leonov, Alexey 87, 91
life
   on Earth 28
   extraterrestrial 124–5
   on Mars 32–3
   origins of 29
liftoff 96
light
   bending 70
   from stars 76–7
   speed of 68–9
light-years 68–9
lightning towers 95
Lippershey, Hans 85
Lovell, Jim 86–7, 114
Lunar Module 96, 97
lunar rovers 93

M

M87 74
main sequence stars 67
Makemake 37
mantle 26
Mariner 2 59
Mars 25, 26
 exploration 121
 life on 32–3
 space suits for 101
 water on 33
 weather 32
massive stars 72
matter 12
 black holes 70
Mercury 26, 44
The Mercury 7 90
mesosphere 11
metals 126
meteor showers 48–9
meteorites 46–7
meteoroids 45–6
meteors 46–9
mice 88
microgravity 108
microphones 21, 100
Milky Way 9, 14, 15
 shape of 74–5
 size of 68–9
 supernovas 73
Mimas 35
Miranda 44
mission control 112–13
Mitchell, Edgar 92
Moon 15, 77
 distance from Earth 130
 experiments 92, 93
 getting to 96–7
 landings 87, 91, 92–3, 97, 121
 mining 127
 orbit of Earth 18–19
 phases of 40–41
 return to 130–31
 temperature 17
 two sides of 41
moons
 asteroids 44, 53
 dwarf planets 36, 37, 44
 planets 44–5

N

NASA 59, 69, 102
navigation 9
nebulas 64–5
Neptune 26
 giant dark spots 31
 rings 35
 temperature 17
neutron stars 73
neutrons 12
New Horizons 121
NGC 1569 74
night sky 76–7
nucleus
 comets 50
 galaxies 75

O

Oberth, Hermann 94
Olympus Mons (Mars) 32
orange subgiants 67
orbits 18–19, 25, 69
Orion 77

P

Paris 54
Perseid meteor shower 49
Philae lander 51, 120
Pillars of Creation 65
planetary nebulas 73
planets 24–5, 77
 composition of 26–7
 outside solar system 78–9
Pluto 36–7
 exploration 120, 121
 moons 44
poles 31, 33, 56
protons 12
Proxima Centauri 62

Q

quasars 80–81

R

radio receivers 125
radio telescopes 124
raw materials 28, 29
reentry 96, 104–5
red dwarfs 67
red giants 67, 72
red supergiants 67, 72
rescue units 101
rings
 Saturn 34–5
 Uranus, Neptune, and Jupiter 35
robots 8, 121
rockets 122
 launching 94–5, 96, 115
 new 131
 space shuttle 102–3
rocky planets 25, 26
rogue planets 78
Rosetta spacecraft 51
Russia 90–91

S

satellites 18, 118–19, 123
Saturn 25, 26
 auroras 56
 exploration 54–5
 Great White Spot 31
 moons 44–5
 rings 34–5
Schmitt, Harrison 92
scientific experiments 107
scientists, rocket 94
Scott, David 92

SETI (Search for Extra-Terrestrial Intelligence) 124–5
Shepard, Alan 92
shooting stars 48–9
solar panels 106, 118
solar system 14, 15, 22–59
    exploration of 120–21
    what is the solar system? 24–5
sound 20–21
Soviet Union 90–91
Soyuz 104, 106, 115
space
    cleaning up 123
    distance traveled in 120–21
    sound in 20–21
    temperatures in 16–17
    vacations in 128–9
    what is space? 8–9
    where does space begin? 10–11
space exploration 8, 82–131
space junk 122–3
space mining 126–7
Space Race 90–91
Space Shuttle 102–3, 105
spacecraft
    distance traveled 120–21
    mission control 112–13
    speed 69

space suits 98, 100–101, 131
space walks 21, 87, 91, 98, 100, 101, 107
SpaceX 131
spiders 88
spiral galaxies 74
splashdown 96, 114, 115
Sputnik 1 and *2* 90
star clusters 9
stardust 29
stars
    death of 29, 72–3
    formation of 9, 13, 63, 64–5
    number of 62–3
    position of 9
    twinkling 76–7
    types of 66–7
stellar nurseries 9, 63, 72
storms 30, 31
Stratollite 129
stratosphere 11
Sun 14, 15, 25, 67
    planetary orbits 18
    temperature 16
supernovas 16, 783
Swigert, Jack 114

T

tails (comets) 50–51
tardigrades 88
teeth, brushing 111
telescopes 8, 84–5
television 119

Tempel-Tuttle comet 49
temperature control system 107
temperatures 16–17
Tereshkova, Valentina 86, 91
thermosphere 10
time (black holes) 70
Titan 44, 54
Tito, Dennis 128
toilets 101, 111
Tombaugh, Clyde 36
Tombaugh Regio 36
tourists, space 128–9
trojans 52
troposphere 11

U

underwear 101
United States 90–91, 92
universe 6–21
    black holes 70
    expanding 12, 13, 14
    number of stars in 62–3
    origin of 12–13
    size of 14–15
Uranus 26
    rings 35
    temperature 16

V

vacations, in space 128–9
vacuum 20–21

Venus 26, 44
    conditions on 58–9
    temperature 17, 58
Venus Express 59
Vesta 52
Virgin Galactic 129
volcanoes 54, 58
Vostok 1 86, 91
Voyager 1 and *2* 120, 125

W

water, liquid 28, 29, 33, 79
weather satellites 118
weightlessness 98, 108–9
Westerlund 2 9
white dwarfs 67, 73
winds 30
World View Enterprises 129
wormholes 70

Y

Yepun telescope 84
Young, John 92

Z

Zvezda module 107

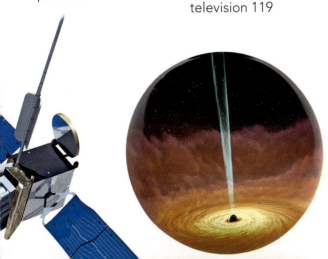

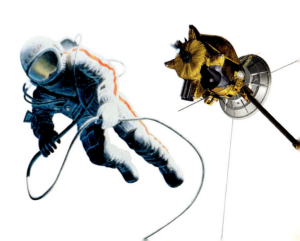

Acknowledgments

DORLING KINDERSLEY would like to thank: Alex Beeden for proofreading, Helen Peters for the index, and Peter Bond for consulting. We would also like to thank Dr. Matt Burleigh, University of Leicester, for his help and advice on stars.

Smithsonian Enterprises
Product Development Manager Kealy Gordon
Director, Licensed Publishing Jill Corcoran
DMM, Ecom and D-to-C Janet Archer
President Carol LeBlanc

The publisher would like to thank the following for their kind permission to reproduce their photographs:

(Key: a-above; b-below/bottom; c-center; f-far; l-left; r-right; t-top)

4 Dorling Kindersley: Andy Crawford (cra). **5 Alamy Stock Photo:** ITAR-TASS Photo Agency (br). **NASA:** Sandra Joseph and Kevin O'Connell (c). **6 ESA / Hubble:** NASA, ESA, the Hubble Heritage Team (STScI / AURA), A. Nota (ESA / STScI), and the Westerlund 2 Science Team (bl). **6-7 NASA:** (t). **8 Dorling Kindersley:** Andy Crawford (cl); NASA (c). **NASA:** JPL-Caltech / MSSS (clb). **8-9 ESA / Hubble:** NASA, ESA, the Hubble Heritage Team (STScI / AURA), A. Nota (ESA / STScI), and the Westerlund 2 Science Team. **11 ESA:** / ESA (fcra). **NASA. 12 NASA:** JPL / STScI Hubble Deep Field Team (bl). **14 NASA. 15 NASA. 17 NASA. 18 Alamy Stock Photo:** JG Photography (bl). **NASA. 19 Dorling Kindersley:** Jamie Marshall and Jamie Marshall. **20-21 NASA. 21 NASA:** NASA / JPL-Caltech (cra). **22-23 Alamy Stock Photo:** Stocktrek Images, Inc. **23 NASA:** NASA / JPL (ca). **25 NASA:** NASA / JPL-Caltech (cra); NASA / JPL-Caltech / STScI (cla). **27 NASA:** NASA / CXC / SAO / K. Poppenhaeger et al; Illustration: NASA / CXC / M. Weiss (cla); NASA / Ames / JPL-Caltech (cl). **28 Alamy Stock Photo:** David Fleetham (bl). **28-29 NASA. 29 NASA:** NASA / ESA / Hubble (cra). **30 NASA. 31 Alamy Stock Photo:** World History Archive (cra). Getty Images: NASA-JPL-Caltech - Voyager / digital version by Science Faction (cr). **32 NASA:** JPL-Caltech / Univ. of Arizona (cl). **33 ESA:** ESA / DLR / FU Berlin (G. Neukum) (br). **34-35 NASA:** NASA / JPL. **36 NASA:** NASA / JHUAPL / SwRI (cb). **37 NASA. 38 NASA:** NASA / SDO / AIA / Goddard Space Flight Center (c). **38-39 NASA:** NASA / SDO. **39 NASA:** NASA / SDO / HMI (bc). **40-41 Dreamstime.com:** Patryk Kosmider (b). **41 Dorling Kindersley:** NASA (ca). **NASA:** NASA / Goddard / Arizona State University. (c). **42 NASA:** NASA / Bill Ingalls (bl); NASA / SDO, AIA (bc). **42-43 Alamy Stock Photo:** Simon Stirrup. **44 NASA:** NASA / JPL / University of Arizona / University of Idaho (bc) (bl). **44-45 Getty Images:** NASA / Roger Ressmeyer / Corbis / VCG (t). **45 Getty Images:** Stocktrek RF (cb). **NASA:** NASA / JPL / University of Arizona (tr); NASA / JPL-Caltech / GSFC / Univ. of Arizona (crb). **46-47 Alamy Stock Photo:** Sindre Ellingsen (b). **47 Dreamstime.com:** Metschurat (ca); Nikkytok (cra). **48-49 Getty Images:** Haitong Yu (b). **49 Alamy Stock Photo:** RGB Ventures (cra); ZUMA Press, Inc. (cr). **50-51 Alamy Stock Photo:** James Thew. **51 NASA:** ESA (bc). **52 NASA:** NASA / JPL-Caltech / UCLA / MPS / DLR / IDA (b). **53 NASA:** NASA / JPL (cra); NASA / JPL-Caltech / UCLA / MPS / DLR / IDA (c). **54 NASA:** J. N. Williams, International Space Station 13 Crew, NASA (bc); JPL (clb); NASA / JSC Gateway to Astronaut Photography of Earth (b). **54-55 NASA:** NASA/JPL-Caltech/Space Science Institute. **56 NASA:** NASA / JPL / ASI / University of Arizona / University of Leicester (cl); NASA, ESA, and J. Nichols University of Leicester (bl). **56-57 Alamy Stock Photo:** Stocktrek Images, Inc. **58 NASA:** NASA / JPL (cb). **59 ESA:** (cr). **NASA:** NASA / JPL (cra). **60-61 ESA / Hubble:** NASA, ESA / Hubble and the Hubble Heritage Team. **61 NASA:** NASA / Ames / JPL-Caltech (tc). **62 ESA / Hubble:** ESA / Hubble & NASA (bl). **62-63 ESA / Hubble:** NASA, ESA, and the Hubble Heritage Team (STScI / AURA)-ESA / Hubble Collaboration. **63 NASA:** JPL / Caltech (crb). **64-65 Getty Images:** Visuals Unlimited, Inc. / Dr. Robert Gendler. **65 ESA / Hubble:** NASA, ESA, M. Livio and the Hubble 20th Anniversary Team (STScI) (cra); NASA, ESA / Hubble and the Hubble Heritage Team (bc). **NASA:** NASA, ESA, and M. Livio and the Hubble 20th Anniversary Team (STScI) (cr). **67 ESA / Hubble:** NASA, ESA and H. Richer (University of British Columbia) (cra/dwarf). **NASA:** NASA, ESA, and K. Luhman (Penn State University) (cra). **68-69 NASA:** NASA / JPL-Caltech (b). **69 NASA. 70 NASA:** NASA, ESA, and D. Coe, J. Anderson, and R. van der Marel (STScI) (clb). **73 NASA:** NASA / ESA / Johns Hopkins University (cra). **74 ESO:** Chris Mihos (Case Western Reserve University) / ESO (cl). **NASA:** NASA, ESA, Hubble Heritage (STScI / AURA), A. Aloisi (STScI / ESA) et al. (clb). **75 NASA. 76-77 Alamy Stock Photo:** Drew Buckley. **77 Alamy Stock Photo:** Brickley Pix (cra); Dimitar Todorov (cr). **78 ESO:** ESO / L. Calçada / P. Delorme / R. Saito / VVV Consortium (bl). **78-79 NASA:** NASA / Ames / JPL-Caltech. **80 ESA / Hubble:** ESA / Hubble & NASA (bl). **NASA:** -ray (NASA / CXC / SAO / P. Green et al.), Optical (Carnegie Obs. / Magellan / W.Baade Telescope / J.S.Mulchaey et al.) (bc). **82 NASA. 83 Getty Images:** Erik Simonsen (tl). **84-85 ESO:** ESO / B. Tafreshi (twanight. org). **85 Alamy Stock Photo:** GL Archive (cla). **86 Alamy Stock Photo:** ITAR-TASS Photo Agency (bl); SPUTNIK (cr). **NASA. 87 Getty Images:** Rykoff Collection (clb). **NASA. 88 Alamy Stock Photo:** Everett Collection Historical (clb); ITAR-TASS Photo Agency (cb). Dreamstime.com: Sebastian Kaulitzki (tr). **NASA. 89 Alamy Stock Photo:** SPUTNIK. **90 Alamy Stock Photo:** Heritage Image Partnership Ltd (cr). **Getty Images:** Sovfoto / UIG (ca). **NASA. 91 Alamy Stock Photo:** SPUTNIK (bc). **Dorling Kindersley:** Andy Crawford / Bob Gathany (c). **NASA. Science Photo Library:** A.SOKOLOV & A.LEONOV / ASAP (cb). **92 NASA. 92-93 NASA. 93 NASA. 94 Alamy Stock Photo:** Photo Researchers, Inc (cb). Getty Images: SSPL (clb). **94-95 Alamy Stock Photo:** Reuters. **96 NASA. 97 NASA. 98 NASA. 98-99 NASA. 101 NASA. 102-103 NASA:** NASA / Sandra Joseph and Kevin O'Connell. **102 NASA. 103 NASA. 104 NASA. 104-105 Alamy Stock Photo:** NG Images (c). **105 Alamy Stock Photo:** Epa European Pressphoto Agency B.v. (br). **NASA. 107 NASA. 108-109 NASA. 108 NASA. 109 NASA. 110-111 NASA. 111 Getty Images:** Roger Ressmeyer / Corbis / VCG (cra). **NASA. 112 NASA. 112-113 NASA:** Bill Ingalls. **114 NASA. 115 NASA. 116 ESA. NASA:** NASA / Pat Rawlings, SAIC (clb). **116-117 NASA:** NASA / JPL-Caltech / MSSS. **117 NASA:** NASA / JPL / Texas A&M / Cornell (cra). **118 NASA. 118-119 Getty Images:** Erik Simonsen. **119 NASA. 120 ESA:** ESA / Rosetta / MPS for OSIRIS Team MPS / UPD / LAM / IAA / SSO / INTA / UPM / DASP / IDA; context: ESA / Rosetta / NavCam – CC BY-SA IGO 3.0 (bl). **NASA:** JPL (cb). **121 NASA. 122 NASA. 123 NASA. 124-125 iStockphoto.com:** Phototreat (b). **125 NASA:** JPL (ca); NASA / JPL-Caltech / SETI Institute (cra). **Science Photo Library:** (cla). **126-127 Planetary Resources. 127 Getty Images:** Photodisc / StockTrek (tr); Victor Habbick Visions (cra). **NASA:** NASA / Ames / SETI Institute / JPL-Caltech (cr). **128 NASA:** JSC (br); NASA / ESA / K. Retherford / SWRI (bl). **128-129 World View Enterprises, Inc. 129 Getty Images:** Virgin Galactic (cra). **130-131 ESA:** ESA / Foster + Partners. **131 Alamy Stock Photo:** SpaceX (bl). **NASA. 134 Dorling Kindersley:** NASA (bl). **134-135 NASA:** NASA / JPL (c). **136 NASA. 136-137 Dorling Kindersley:** (c). **137 Dorling Kindersley:** Andy Crawford (ca). ESO: ESO / L.Calçada / NASA / JPL-Caltech / UCLA / MPS / DLR / IDA / Steve Albers / N. Risinger (skysurvey.org) (crb). **NASA:** ESA (cb). **138 Alamy Stock Photo:** SPUTNIK (bc). **NASA:** NASA / JPL-Caltech / MSSS (bc, fbr). **140 Dorling Kindersley:** Andy Crawford / Bob Gathany (bc). **141 Getty Images:** Erik Simonsen (fbl). **NASA. Science Photo Library:** A.SOKOLOV & A.LEONOV / ASAP (br)

Endpapers: NASA: ESA, and the Hubble Heritage Team (STScI/AURA)-ESA/Hubble Collaboration; Acknowledgment: D. Gouliermis (Max Planck Institute for Astronomy, Heidelberg).

Cover images: Front and Back: **Science Photo Library:** Lynette Cook t; Front: **Alamy Stock Photo:** James Thew cb; **Dorling Kindersley:** NASA ca; **Dreamstime. com:** TMarchev br; **NASA:** JPL-Caltech t, NASA, ESA, and the Hubble Heritage (STScI / AURA)-ESA / Hubble Collaboration ca/ (spiral), JPL-Caltech / STScI / CXC / UofA / ESA / AURA / JHU c/ (M82), NASA / SDO bl; Back: **123RF.com:** Manjik cr; **Dorling Kindersley:** NASA cb, NASA bl; **Dreamstime.com:** TMarchev tl; **Getty Images:** Erik Simonsen cb/ (satellite); **NASA:** JPL / University of Arizona cra, JPL-Caltech / STScI / CXC / UofA / ESA / AURA / JHU c/ (background), JPL / MSSS tc, Johns Hopkins University Applied Physics Laboratory / Carnegie Institution of Washington cra/ (mercury)

All other images © Dorling Kindersley
For further information see: www.dkimages.com